Behavioural Economics: A Very Short Introduction

VERY SHORT INTRODUCTIONS are for anyone wanting a stimulating and accessible way into a new subject. They are written by experts, and have been translated into more than 45 different languages.

The series began in 1995, and now covers a wide variety of topics in every discipline. The VSI library now contains over 500 volumes—a Very Short Introduction to everything from Psychology and Philosophy of Science to American History and Relativity—and continues to grow in every subject area.

Very Short Introductions available now:

ACCOUNTING Christopher Nobes
ADOLESCENCE Peter K. Smith
ADVERTISING Winston Fletcher
AFRICAN AMERICAN RELIGION
  Eddie S. Glaude Jr
AFRICAN HISTORY John Parker and
  Richard Rathbone
AFRICAN RELIGIONS
  Jacob K. Olupona
AGEING Nancy A. Pachana
AGNOSTICISM Robin Le Poidevin
AGRICULTURE Paul Brassley and
  Richard Soffe
ALEXANDER THE GREAT
  Hugh Bowden
ALGEBRA Peter M. Higgins
AMERICAN HISTORY Paul S. Boyer
AMERICAN IMMIGRATION
  David A. Gerber
AMERICAN LEGAL HISTORY
  G. Edward White
AMERICAN POLITICAL HISTORY
  Donald Critchlow
AMERICAN POLITICAL PARTIES
  AND ELECTIONS L. Sandy Maisel
AMERICAN POLITICS
  Richard M. Valelly
THE AMERICAN PRESIDENCY
  Charles O. Jones
THE AMERICAN REVOLUTION
  Robert J. Allison
AMERICAN SLAVERY
  Heather Andrea Williams
THE AMERICAN WEST Stephen Aron

AMERICAN WOMEN'S HISTORY
  Susan Ware
ANAESTHESIA Aidan O'Donnell
ANARCHISM Colin Ward
ANCIENT ASSYRIA Karen Radner
ANCIENT EGYPT Ian Shaw
ANCIENT EGYPTIAN ART AND
  ARCHITECTURE Christina Riggs
ANCIENT GREECE Paul Cartledge
THE ANCIENT NEAR EAST
  Amanda H. Podany
ANCIENT PHILOSOPHY Julia Annas
ANCIENT WARFARE
  Harry Sidebottom
ANGELS David Albert Jones
ANGLICANISM Mark Chapman
THE ANGLO-SAXON AGE John Blair
THE ANIMAL KINGDOM
  Peter Holland
ANIMAL RIGHTS David DeGrazia
THE ANTARCTIC Klaus Dodds
ANTISEMITISM Steven Beller
ANXIETY Daniel Freeman and
  Jason Freeman
THE APOCRYPHAL GOSPELS
  Paul Foster
ARCHAEOLOGY Paul Bahn
ARCHITECTURE Andrew Ballantyne
ARISTOCRACY William Doyle
ARISTOTLE Jonathan Barnes
ART HISTORY Dana Arnold
ART THEORY Cynthia Freeland
ASIAN AMERICAN HISTORY
  Madeline Y. Hsu

Available soon:

For more information visit our website

www.oup.com/vsi/

Michelle Baddeley

BEHAVIOURAL ECONOMICS

A Very Short Introduction

OXFORD
UNIVERSITY PRESS

OXFORD

UNIVERSITY PRESS

Great Clarendon Street, Oxford, OX2 6DP,
United Kingdom

Oxford University Press is a department of the University of Oxford.
It furthers the University's objective of excellence in research, scholarship,
and education by publishing worldwide. Oxford is a registered trade mark of
Oxford University Press in the UK and in certain other countries

Published in the United States of America by Oxford University Press
198 Madison Avenue, New York, NY 10016, United States of America

British Library Cataloguing in Publication Data
Data available

Library of Congress Control Number: 2016950215

ISBN 978-0-19-875499-2

Printed and bound by CPI Group (UK) Ltd, Croydon, CR0 4YY

To my grandmother Irene Baddeley, née Bates,
1916–2009, on the centenary of her birth.
In memory of her practical wisdom and
unstinting support for her granddaughters.

If all the year were playing holidays,
To sport would be as tedious as to work;
But when they seldom come, they wish'd-for come,
And nothing pleaseth but rare accidents.

William Shakespeare, King Henry the 4th,
Part I (Act 1, Scene 2, 173–95)

Contents

Acknowledgements

My thanks go to Joy Mellor, my copy editor, for her enthusiasm, meticulous work on the manuscript, and lots of good suggestions; and also to Dorothy McCarthy—for her thorough proof-reading and for her vote of confidence in the content. Thanks also to all at the Oxford University Press for their help—including Andrea Keegan, for her wise advice and for guiding the proposal through the early stages; Jenny Nugee, for efficiently guiding the manuscript through to publication; Deborah Protheroe, for her help and advice with illustrations; and Ruby Constable, Chloe Mussen, and Martha Cunneen, for their editorial assistance. Thanks also to Saraswathi Ethiraju, for overseeing the production process. The anonymous reviewers of the proposal and first draft also contributed some excellent thoughts and advice, so my thanks to them too, though, as always, errors and omissions remain my own.

My gratitude also goes to all those who took a look at the script—including my family, friends, students, and colleagues. I am particularly grateful to Pete Lunn, for reading the manuscript so thoroughly and making some excellent suggestions; and to Nissy Sombatruang, for her enthusiastic feedback on the first draft, and also for suggesting the Thai examples included in Chapter 2. A special mention goes to my former UCL student,

Josephine Pletts, for suggesting that a *Very Short Introduction* might be a nice writing project to consider in the first place.

A final thank you to my husband Chris—for his generosity, warmth, and patient support for all that I do.

List of illustrations

Chapter 1
Economics and behaviour

Behavioural economics is a hot topic. Behavioural economics research is regularly featured in the top academic journals in economics and science. It has a high profile on social media, and journalists regularly write about the new books and research emerging in the field. Governments and other policy-makers, from all over the world, are embedding insights from behavioural economics into their policy designs, as, increasingly, are more mainstream economists when designing their models.

What is behavioural economics and why so much interest? Behavioural economics extends economic principles by allowing that our decisions are affected by social and psychological influences, as well as a rational calculation of benefits and costs. It also broadens economics, making it more accessible to a wider audience. Undeniably, economics is a critically important subject because it is all about our welfare—at an individual level, nationally and internationally, and for our children and future generations. But it is also perceived by many to be an esoteric, technocratic subject. People without economics qualifications struggle to understand the key concepts. Behavioural economics has the potential to change this because it strikes many as being much more interesting. It provides a more intuitive and less mathematical account of our decision-making.

Behavioural economics is also interesting because of the pluralism and diversity in its underlying principles. Behavioural economists bring economics together with insights from a wide range of other disciplines, for example psychology (especially social psychology), sociology, neuroscience, and evolutionary biology. Using this multidisciplinary blend of ideas, behavioural economists enrich our understanding of economic and financial behaviour, without necessarily abandoning the analytical power often associated with conventional economics.

Why is behavioural economics different?

Most economists describe people as mathematical calculators—able easily and accurately to add up the money costs and benefits of their choices in pounds and pence, dollars and cents—and without worrying about what others around them are doing. Most economists start with the presumption that economic problems emerge, not because people as individuals are fallible, but because of failures in markets and their supporting institutions. Barriers stop small firms from entering markets and allow large, rich monopolies to dominate markets, elevate prices, and constrain production. Information may be distorted. There may be missing markets—for example there are no natural markets for cigarette smoke and pollution, so prices do not fully capture the balance of benefits and costs of smoking or pollution.

Rationality in behavioural economics

While conventional economists direct their attention away from limits to rationality, behavioural economists do not assume that people are super-rational beings. Instead they focus on some limits to rational decision-making. Many behavioural economists draw on some ideas from Herbert Simon who was a psychologist and computer scientist as well as Nobel Laureate in Economics. He is famous for his concept of *bounded rationality*, capturing the idea that we are limited and bounded by various constraints when we are deciding. Cognitive constraints may limit our ability to choose the best strategies. Limits on memory or numerical processing ability mean that sometimes we are forced towards a particular option because we do not have the information or cognitive processing time or power to consider other options.

Behavioural economists develop other conceptions of rationality too. Another Nobel Laureate, Vernon L. Smith, develops the concept of *ecological rationality*. He hypothesizes that rationality is malleable because it is determined by the contexts and circumstances in which we find ourselves. Similarly, Gerd Gigerenzer argues that we are driven by a practical rationality—in the real world we have to decide quickly and 'frugally'—we do not have time to collect lots of information, or to apply complex decision-making rules. We decide quickly and simply. Often this works well, but other times it leads us into systematic behavioural biases.

Another economist with interesting insights about what it means to be rational is Harvey Leibenstein, who developed the concept of *selective rationality*—similar to Vernon L. Smith's ecological rationality. We choose when to be super-rational and sometimes we do take full account of all available information. At other times, however, we may decide to stick with the status quo, and remain in what Leibenstein describes as *inert areas*. This makes our choices 'sticky'. We do not always adapt our behaviours effectively to new circumstances. When our behaviour is sticky Leibenstein argues that there are two explanations: either we have decided that the costs of changing choices are too high or, in other cases, we are just too lazy and apathetic to change.

So behavioural economists have a complex range of views about what it means to be rational. Mostly, they allow that our rationality is variable and dependent on the circumstances in which we find ourselves. When we do not have access to good information, when we are in a hurry, when we are facing cognitive constraints or social influences—then we might be led into decisions that, in a perfect world with plenty of time and information, we could improve.

Data constraints

While this form of economics has plenty of potential, a key constraint for behavioural economists lies in finding relevant and reliable data. Behavioural economists often use experiments to collect data—in contrast to the traditional empirical approach in economics of using econometric, statistical methods to analyse published, historical data, collected by governments and international statistical agencies.

Often behavioural economists are trying to infer something about people's thinking and feeling processes, not yet knowing exactly what is driving people's choices. Standard economic data sources are not so helpful in this because traditionally economic data is about observed choices and outcomes (e.g. employment and unemployment statistics in a macroeconomic context). Behavioural economists can rely on survey data—for example, questions about people's perceptions of their own happiness and well-being are being incorporated into household surveys. But survey data has limitations—how does a researcher identify a representative sample? How does a researcher cope with untruthful or ill-informed answers to survey questions?

Experimental data

Laboratory experiments are probably the most common data source for behavioural economists. The problem with many lab experiments is that they are conducted in universities, often with university students as experimental participants. Students' choices in experiments may not correlate well with real-world choices, in which case this experimental data will lack *external validity*—the experimental findings will not translate well to the real world. So, for example, if a student participates in a trading experiment, their observed choices may have little connection with how real traders would behave, because students have limited knowledge and experience, and are likely to be less strongly motivated to succeed.

Another significant obstacle to reliable experimental data is experimental design. Experimenters can find it difficult to construct a 'clean' controlled experiment in economics. Some economists have criticized early findings from behavioural economists on the basis that the experimental participants' responses demonstrated confusion about what they were supposed to be doing, and the behavioural anomalies identified were not genuine systematic biases. There are ethical trade-offs too. What should an experimenter be allowed to put his or her participants through, especially if they are, for example, vulnerable hospital patients? Is it legitimate to deceive experimental participants; and is it possible to design an artificial experiment that involves no deception at all?

Online experiments are enabled by tools such as Survey Monkey, Prolific Academic, and Task Rabbit as well as, increasingly, mobile apps. These methods are cheap and can be a very quick and easy way to get large batches of experimental data. But how does the researcher ensure that they are using a representative sample? How do they deal with the problem of unmotivated participants who may just tap computer keys at random, being most interested in simply earning money from the exercise? Motivating experimental participants to behave realistically in experimental trials is a significant problem for behavioural economists, especially as academic research budgets are often limited.

Neuroscientific data and neuroeconomics

Combined with experimental data, neuroscientific data can help illuminate some key influences. There is a wide range of neuroscientific techniques. Choices made by brain-lesion patients can help to inform us about which brain areas are implicated in economic decisions. Similarly, brain-imaging techniques (e.g. functional magnetic resonance imaging, or fMRI) can capture how our economic decisions correlate with neural responses in specific brain regions. Another technique increasing in popularity is transcranial magnetic stimulation (TMS), which involves zapping specific areas of the brain and seeing how people's choices subsequently change as a consequence of this temporary interference. There are other simpler and cheaper neuroscientific tools too, including monitoring physiological responses (heart rate, pulse rate, etc.); or measuring hormone levels (e.g. oxytocin levels in studies of trust; and testosterone levels in studies of financial risk-taking).

The key advantage for neuroscientific data is that it is relatively objective. With surveys, respondents may be expressing a possibly unreliable subjective opinion; or they may have reasons to lie or manipulate their responses. It is much harder, if not impossible, for an experimental participant to control the physiological responses measured using neuroscientific tools, though this does not remove an experimenter's bias in their experimental designs.

Natural experiments and randomized controlled trials (RCTs)

One problem with standard experiments, as mentioned earlier, is that they can lack external validity. *Natural experiments*, if we can find them, are a solution—natural experimental data that emerges by chance from real-world events and behaviours. One example is a study by economists DellaVigna and Malmendier of gym membership and attendance data, described in Chapter 6, showing that many people pay large sums of money for gym memberships that they rarely use. But good data from natural experiments are rare and we would not get far if we relied only on these data sources. One solution is to use RCTs. These are experimental methods commonly used in clinical trials to identify treatment effects: impacts on experimental participants receiving a trial treatment are compared with impacts on experimental participants in a control group receiving just a placebo.

Behavioural economists borrow these methods to compare a control group's responses to a treatment group's responses. However, as experimenters would find it difficult to design a socio-economic equivalent of a placebo, the control group in these studies receives no treatment at all. This means that with behavioural economics RCTs it is not possible to establish whether or not it is the intervention itself that is changing behaviours, or just some economic equivalent of a placebo effect from people responding positively to any intervention regardless of how genuinely effective it might be. Nonetheless, RCTs are now widely used by behavioural development economists to study impacts of development interventions on socio-economic outcomes.

Key themes

There is an enormous literature in behavioural economics—it could fill a library of its own. In this Very Short Introduction, we will focus on a few key themes, each explored in the following chapters: what motivates us; how we are affected by social influences; how and why we make mistakes; how we judge and misjudge risk; our tendency to short-termism; and how personality, mood, and emotions drive our choices and decisions. Once these key behavioural, microeconomic principles have been explored, we will explore how this can all be brought together in behavioural macroeconomics. Then we will turn to the policy implications and lessons adopted by public policy-makers—illustrated by a number of examples of influential policy studies based around behavioural economic insights.

Chapter 2
Motivation and incentives

If you were to watch some economists talking together—at a conference, for example—it would not take long for someone to mention 'incentives'. Incentives are the fundamental driver in economic analysis. Incentives encourage people to work harder and better. They encourage businesses to provide more and better products. Economists usually assume that money is the main incentive, and there is no doubt that money can provide an objective (though not necessarily accurate or fair) measure of value. Money motivates us in much of our ordinary lives. It determines the prices we pay or do not pay for the goods and services we buy, and the wages we earn or do not earn. Higher prices and wages reward better, more productive decision-making. Monetary incentives underpin the markets that coordinate the choices of many different people and businesses.

As a behavioural economist, I would not argue against the idea that prices and money are powerful incentives motivating us to work harder and better, but rather that a complex range of other socio-economic and psychological factors drive our decision-making too. We are motivated by far more than just money. As an academic, perhaps I am not paid as well as I might be in the private sector. If I look at my lifetime's earnings, perhaps the fact that I have a generous pension and far more job security explains why I am not maximizing my earnings today. But there is something else going on too because there are parts of my job that I genuinely enjoy—they tap into my other non-monetary motivations. Sometimes, I think that if I won the lottery and so did not have to worry about having enough money to live, I would not give up my job. Sometimes my job gives me a pleasure all of its own, quite apart from the money I am paid.

Intrinsic versus extrinsic motivations and incentives

We see this every day in our working lives—at work we are motivated by a number of different monetary and non-monetary rewards. Most people want to be paid for the work they do, but some people do not work just for money. Some people may also be incentivized by social rewards, such as social approval, that come from working hard and having a well-respected job. Some people are driven by moral incentives—for example, those who work for charities. Others just enjoy what they do and so work at it even though it is not well paid—for example, many artists.

Behavioural economists capture these wider influences on our decisions and choices by categorizing two broad groups of incentives and motivations: *intrinsic* and *extrinsic*.

Extrinsic motivation

Extrinsic motivations capture the incentives and rewards external to us as individuals—for example, when the world and the people around us encourage us to do something we would otherwise be reluctant to do. Then our actions must be driven by something outside ourselves: we need extrinsic motivation in the form of an incentive. A common and powerful incentive is money: we work because we are paid a wage or salary. A more powerful external incentive is physical threat. But extrinsic motivations can also come from non-monetary incentives—for example, social rewards such as social approval and social success. Higher wages, good exam results, prizes and awards, and social approval are all external rewards.

Intrinsic motivation

Intrinsic motivations reflect the influence of our internal goals and attitudes. An internal response sometimes encourages us to make an effort—for our own sake, not because we are driven by some external reward. When we are intrinsically motivated by something inside ourselves—whether it be professional pride, a sense of duty, loyalty to a cause, enjoyment from solving a puzzle, or pleasure in being physically active—then we do not need external incentives. When we play a game of chess or cards, or a computer game, we enjoy the challenge—and that enjoyment is internally driven from within us. Many artisans and craftspeople enjoy their job and take pride in it, and, while the money they are paid is not irrelevant because they and their families need money to live, the money is just one of many motivating factors.

Crowding out

Extrinsic and intrinsic motivations are not independent of each other. Extrinsic motivations can *crowd out* our intrinsic motivations. This occurs when our intrinsic motivations are dampened by external rewards. Some experiments have shown how this can happen. One set of studies to capture the crowding out of intrinsic motivation involved experimenters asking university students to solve a series of puzzles. Students were sorted randomly into two groups: one group was paid; the other group was not. Surprisingly, some of the students in the second group did better than students in the first. The unpaid students were enjoying the intellectual challenge; the paid students were perhaps demotivated by relatively low rates of pay. When the students were paid, they were distracted from enjoying the intellectual challenge of the task (the intrinsic motivation), and were focused instead on whether or not they were being paid enough (the extrinsic motivation). Other studies have also shown that small payments can be demotivating, leading to worse performance than when there is no payment at all, because small payments crowd out intrinsic motivation without offering sufficient external incentives to fully develop an extrinsic motivation.

Extrinsic incentives and disincentives affect our ordinary lives too and often in surprising ways, as shown in a study of nursery schools by economists Uri Gneezy and Aldo Rustichini. A nursery in Israel had a problem with parents arriving late to collect their children. Teachers were often forced to wait behind after closing time to care for the children until their parents turned up. This was costly and disruptive for the nursery and its teachers, so the nursery managers decided to introduce a fine as a deterrent.

The impact was surprising: with a fine, *more* parents started arriving late—not fewer. The researchers postulated that this might be because parents were not interpreting the fine as a deterrent. They were interpreting it as a price. The nursery was providing an additional service—looking after children after normal school hours. Some parents were willing to pay for this additional service, and because the parents perceived this as a reciprocal and mutually beneficial arrangement (the nursery was getting more money, after all) they did not feel the guilt that had previously stopped them turning up late too often. Again, this might reflect crowding out of intrinsic motivations. Before the fine, many parents might have been intrinsically motivated to be cooperative and considerate in turning up on time as often as possible. After the fine had been introduced, their perception of the situation changed—they were just paying for the luxury of arriving late. The monetary disincentive of the fine was crowding out the intrinsic motivation to be a cooperative parent.

Blood donations are another important example of when and how extrinsic motivations crowd out intrinsic motivations. Low levels of blood donation are a big problem in many countries and some economists have explored new ways to encourage more people to donate blood. The obvious economic solution is to pay donors. However, when researchers experimented with introducing payments for blood donation to encourage more donations, they found that it had a perverse and unexpected effect: it lowered rather than raised people's willingness to donate. One explanation could be that the extrinsic motivation from monetary payments undermined donors' intrinsic motivation to be good citizens.

Pro-social choices and image motivation

Charitable donations are another example of the complex interplay between extrinsic and intrinsic motivations. Some people give to charity because they feel a moral or religious obligation. Others give to charity because it makes them look good. Many of us probably do it for a mixture of reasons. When Mark Zuckerberg and his wife donated most of their fortune to mark the birth of their first child, was this choice about an intrinsic moral motivation to help the world? Or was their choice about being admired by others as generous philanthropists, and a way to enhance their social reputations?

Behavioural economists have studied these charitable motivations in more depth, exploring when and how extrinsic rewards can 'spoil' the reputational value of pro-social behaviours such as generosity and philanthropy. They find that when people accrue personal benefits from their 'generosity' and information about these benefits is made publicly available then people are less likely to be generous. One of our young researchers has told me that, in Thailand, when there is a festival or a funeral, people put the money they want to donate into an envelope with their names on the envelope. Alternatively, they give money directly to a collector, who notes the donor details and amounts donated. Organizers then announce publicly and loudly, through loud-hailers installed around the village, the names of donors and the amounts donated. Apparently, villagers within a kilometre radius can hear the announcements and children are instructed to pay attention to the names.

These types of behaviour show that our social reputations are important to us, particularly in the context of generosity and charity, and they illustrate a social type of extrinsic motivation: *image motivation*. Some of our choices reflect the fact that we want to boost our reputations and improve our image.

To explore the impact of image motivation, Dan Ariely and colleagues explored how people's pro-social choices are affected when external rewards are visible to others. He and his team started with the premise that donations to charitable causes are driven by image motivation and are a way of signalling to others that you are a good person. However, if additional benefits are available as a reward for philanthropy, and if everyone can see our charitable choices being rewarded in other ways, then the image motivation is weakened. When it is public knowledge that we have given to charity, we signal to others that we are good people. But if others can see that we are earning personal benefits from our generosity, then the social signalling value of our generosity is diluted.

To test these ideas, Dan Ariely and his team designed a 'Click for Charity' experiment. In their experiment, they assigned people randomly to one of two charities: a 'good' charity—the American Red Cross; and a 'bad' charity—the National Rifle Association. Then they asked their experimental participants to perform a task requiring very little effort—pressing 'x' or 'z' on a keyboard, for example. For all the experimental participants, performance in this simple key-pressing task was rewarded by donations to their charity. To test the impact of additional private benefits, the experimental participants were divided into two groups: some of them were able to earn money for themselves if they performed well; others were given no additional payments at all. These two groups were divided again according to whether their performance in the 'Click for Charity' task was made public to the rest of the experimental group or whether it remained private, known only to the individual participants and the experimenters.

Unsurprisingly, Ariely and his team found that the groups making the most effort, measured by the number of key-presses, were those performing for the 'good' charity (the Red Cross). More surprisingly, the participants exhibited some complex interactions of extrinsic motivations in terms of money incentives versus image motivation. The best performing group was not paid money, but its efforts were made public. Image motivation is the most likely explanation for their superior performance—they worked hard to enhance their social reputation because their efforts would be made public. The worst performing group also received no additional money incentive, but their efforts remained private. They had nothing to gain: no extra income and no social value because no-one would know whether or not they had made an effort. In fact, what reason did this latter group have to make any effort at all given that their rewards were neither social nor monetary?

The most interesting finding was seen in those who were earning additional private income for their efforts. They worked less hard than the best performing group (i.e. those who received no private income, but their efforts were made public). From this study, it seems that image motivation is a more powerful incentive than monetary payments, at least in the context of charitable donations. But image motivation does not completely crowd out conventional monetary incentives: for the two groups being paid, those whose efforts were also made public did still perform better than those whose efforts remained private. Both image motivation and monetary payments played a role in incentivizing effort.

Overall, the findings from this and other studies confirm what most economists would probably predict: monetary incentives can encourage anonymous giving. Perhaps this is why tax breaks for charitable giving—GiftAid in the UK, for example—work well in the real world. But in some cases monetary incentives do not work. Many people do not take advantage of tax breaks on their charitable giving, but this could reflect the transaction costs involved in claiming tax rebates and/or procrastination—a theme explored in Chapter 6. These studies suggest another, potentially more powerful, policy lesson: if people's charitable impulses can be made public more easily then the inclination towards philanthropy will increase, and this effect might be more powerful than conventional monetary incentives such as tax breaks. In a world dominated by social media where we have an opportunity to publicize our good character and generosity, then charitable giving is more likely.

These findings also connect to debates about executive pay in the charitable sector. Paying chief executives of charities high commercial salaries might have a counter-productive impact on the charity—both in terms of the people attracted to these jobs and the negative perceptions of potential donors. If a charity's chief executive is apparently strongly motivated by monetary incentives, this runs counter to the expected ethos for charity work, and so the charity's reputation is likely to suffer—potential donors like myself may decide that this is not the sort of charity we would wish to support.

Motivating work

Incentives and motivations, both intrinsic and extrinsic, are also powerful influences in our working lives. Most workers are motivated by interplays of internal and external influences. Extrinsic incentives and motivations include the wages and salaries we earn, and also the social approval we get when we are employed—especially if it is in a job perceived to be worthy (e.g. medicine or education). Working also reflects intrinsic motivations, for example: we enjoy a challenge; it is satisfying to be doing something; or we are motivated by personal ambition.

these insights from behavioural economics about incentives and motivation can link into one of the most powerful and influential approaches to understanding wages and employees' efforts and productivity—*efficiency wage theory*. Efficiency wage theory captures how economic and socio-psychological influences motivate effort at work. Efficiency wage theorists explain what constitutes an efficient wage—defined as the wage that minimizes a firm's labour costs. If raising a worker's wage leads to a more than proportionate increase in the worker's productivity then the firm's profits will rise, not fall. For example, if a worker's wage is increased by 1 per cent but the higher wage encourages them to work much harder so that they produce 2 per cent more output, then labour costs per unit of output have fallen. All things being equal, profits will rise.

A simultaneous rise in wages and profits can be explained partly in terms of standard economic concepts. If an employee is paid well, they will value their job more, will not want to lose it, and so they will work harder. In very poor economies, paying more might help workers to afford better food, shelter, healthcare, and clothing—so, physically, they will be stronger and more able to work longer and harder, and take less time away from work through illness. Paying more might deter strike activity amongst unionized workers.

However, higher wages motivate employees to work hard not just because of the money benefits but also because of social and psychological rewards and incentives, including the impact that being treated well has on an employee's trust and loyalty. When your boss treats you better than you expect, you will want to reciprocate by being a better worker. The employer–employee relationship is not just about monetary exchange. It is also about social and psychological incentives and drivers, including loyalty, trust, and reciprocity. George Akerlof and colleagues describe this as a form of 'gift exchange'. My boss treats me well and pays me well, so I return the favour by working harder.

Many of us may have experienced this in our working lives. The jobs we do over our lifetimes, and the contrast between our best and worst jobs, can illustrate how workers' motivations are complex. Imagine that you are working in a shop, filled with things you might usually like to buy—sports equipment, good food, or nice shoes. To start with, you are more likely to enjoy your job and work hard. If, in addition, your boss treats you well and your job is intrinsically satisfying, then you are likely to work without close monitoring, which saves your boss supervision costs—you and your boss trust each other and so you show initiative in working hard. You might also spread the word amongst your friends and other networks, which will help your boss to attract good new workers without having to advertise very widely. This will save your boss labour search costs, and also reduces their risk of hiring a shirker.

So incorporating non-monetary incentives into the analysis of labour markets is not just about our charitable impulses. It also has important implications for businesses and policy-makers. Lowering wages does not necessarily increase business profits; paying a *higher* wage, however, might increase profits. Efficiency wage theory also brings insights into policy debates about minimum wages and the *living wage* (i.e. a wage that allows workers to meet the local cost of basic living). Higher, fairer wages can benefit everyone—employers and employees. If paying a higher wage motivates workers to work harder for a business both inside and outside work, then the case for better pay is easier to defend.

This chapter has shown how behavioural economists take basic economic insights—for example, that people respond to incentives—and define the concepts (incentives and motivations, in this case) more broadly, allowing that socio-psychological influences play a role too. Once we allow that our choices and behaviours are affected by a wider set of social, economic, and psychological motivations, this significantly changes the standard economic prescriptions for better performance. How we

nk about our own and others' image and social reputations
fects our donations to charity and our responses to fines. Our
social interactions with others drive our performance at work as
well as our firm's profits. Markets capture the interactions of
people, and while it is clear that people respond to monetary
incentives, there is a range of other powerful influences too. As
individuals, employees, employers, policy-makers, and citizens,
insights from behavioural economics can help us to develop a
much richer understanding of the complex motivations driving
our choices and efforts, and their consequences.

This chapter has explored some of the influences on our choices
and decisions, including social influences that reflect some of the
extrinsic motivations that drive us. In Chapter 3, we will see how
people are affected by a wider range of social influences—including
aversion to unequal outcomes, trust and reciprocity, social learning,
and peer pressure.

Chapter 3
Social lives

In Chapter 2, we explored the ways in which our economic and financial decisions are determined by a range of factors, apart from money. Most economic theories start by assuming that we are independent and self-interested creatures, who do not look to others when deciding what to do. All things being equal, anonymous markets are the best way to coordinate economic activity and ensure that consumers and producers get the best, most mutually beneficial, deal possible.

The standard assumption in economics is that we all behave as if others do not actually exist as individuals. We are affected by other people only indirectly, because their decisions about supply and demand drive market prices. This leaves out an important dimension of people's economic lives. Prices are impersonal and by only focusing on prices in economic analysis, economists can easily forget the importance of human relationships and social interactions in economic decision-making. There are many ways in which economic choices are affected by the others around us. Literatures from social psychology and sociology are illuminating in showing how and why this happens. In this chapter we will explore some of the main ways in which social influences drive behaviour.

We care about others around us, or not; they care about us, or not. We worry about fairness and tend to prefer fair outcomes over unfair outcomes. We are also inclined to trust others in some situations, and they sometimes trust us in return. When other people are trustworthy and treat us well, we are more likely to reciprocate by trusting and being trustworthy in return. For example, if my colleagues help me out with my lecturing and administrative tasks, then I will feel more willing to help them with their lecturing and administrative tasks. This interplay between trust and reciprocity is a key element in many of the cooperative and collaborative activities that we undertake every day—everything from collaborative teamwork when we are working or studying, through to the altruism we show when donating to charity, and the cooperation that is necessary for family life, community projects, and political movements to succeed.

The analysis of trust and reciprocity in behavioural economics starts from the insight that people do not generally like to see unequal outcomes. People do not like to be treated unfairly, and they do not like to see others being treated unfairly either. If we feel that we are being treated unfairly then we are less likely to trust and reciprocate. This key element in our social interactions links our preference for fairness with how we feel we are doing relative to others. We do not like situations when others seem to be doing much better or worse than we are because we do not like inequitable outcomes. Behavioural economists call this preference *inequity aversion*.

There are two main types of inequity aversion both of which can be captured by thinking about a banker meeting a homeless person on the streets of London. The banker may be distressed to see someone suffering from poverty—he would prefer that living standards were more equal—if so, he is feeling *advantageous inequity aversion*. The banker is coming from a position of advantage, but perhaps he does not want to see others suffering from a much lower standard of living, and would like to see a fairer outcome for the homeless person. The homeless person also does not want to suffer from inequity. She would prefer to have enough money to afford a safe and comfortable place to live—her predicament is unfair and she will experience a preference known as *disadvantageous inequity aversion*; from her position of disadvantage, she does not want to be relatively worse off than others around her.

While both are experiencing a similar aversion to unequal outcomes, it is likely that the beggar is far more concerned about her unequal position than the banker: people are much more affected by disadvantageous inequity aversion than by advantageous inequity aversion. The banker is likely to feel mild discomfort at seeing a homeless person on the street; the homeless person, however, will be feeling much more unhappy about the inequity.

Our preference for fairness can also explain altruism—for example, when we volunteer or give to charity. We may do this because we enjoy being generous and sometimes get a warm feeling from our generosity. Some experiments show that it is not always about pure altruism, sometimes it is about signalling to others that we are good and generous people. As noted in Chapter 2, people are more likely to give more when their generosity is made public.

Many experimental studies have confirmed that inequity aversion is a strong tendency, not only among humans across most countries and cultures, but also among our primate cousins. The basic experimental game used to test inequity aversion is the *Ultimatum Game*. In its simplest form, this game is played by two players. Player A, the proposer, has a sum—say £100—and can offer whatever amount she likes to Player B—the responder.

the responder rejects the proposer's offer then neither player gets anything, and the proposer has to return the £100 to the experimenter. Non-behavioural economists would probably predict that people will play this game perfectly selfishly and aim to get as much as they can, given what they believe about the other player's strategies. Player A will assume that Player B would prefer £1 to £0 because something is better than nothing. So Player A will make a £1 offer because she thinks that Player B will probably accept it. If Player B does not care what Player A thinks or does, he will prefer £1 to £0 and so will accept Player A's offer. Player A has deduced that Player B will react in this way and therefore offers £1 and keeps £99 for herself.

The Ultimatum Game is one of the most used experiments in behavioural economics—and it has been adapted to test responses to different sums of money, and to explore differences across a wide range of countries and cultures. The experiment has even been used in animal experiments. Chimps playing the game for juice and fruit treats exhibit similar behaviour to humans. Across all these different studies, the robust finding is that real-world behaviour is very different from what most economists might expect: the proposer is often very generous—offering much more than £1 or its equivalent, while the responder is often seen rejecting offers even when offered 40 per cent or more of the total sum available.

Some behavioural economists explain inequity aversion as a type of emotion—a social emotion. Our social situations can lead us to feel particular emotions such as envy, jealousy, and resentment, and there is probably an emotional element when people are treated unfairly in the Ultimatum Game. For example, if the responder (Player B) resents the proposer (Player A) for making a mean offer, then he may be prepared to pay £40+ to punish the proposer. Neuroscientists have used brain-imaging studies to unravel what might be going on with our brains. One study involved imaging the brains of experimental participants in the responder role. Their brain responses suggested that the same neural areas that were activated, for example, when people were disgusted by a bad smell were also activated when people were treated unfairly in the Ultimatum Game. Some neuroscientists and neuroeconomists interpret these findings as evidence that we experience a form of social disgust when others treat us unfairly.

Cooperation, punishment, and social norms

Social norms are another set of social influences that drive our behaviour, and these are often reinforced through peer pressure. Given our social natures, we generally reward (and are rewarded for) pro-social behaviour—if teenagers copy their peers in their choices and habits, then they are probably more likely to be invited to the coolest parties. Conformity has a strong influence and it drives our customs, traditions, and religious life. When driven by blind conformity, social influences are not always benign—for example, when cults form. Cults are an extreme example of destructive social behaviour but conformity has power in more ordinary contexts too. We often compare our own behaviour with what others are doing, and others' behaviour provides us with what behavioural economists call our *social reference points*: we make our own decisions with reference to what we believe to be the average decision of the group. Many organizations, from government policy-makers to those in marketing, use information about our social reference points to leverage more constructive behaviour, for example, or more profits.

Social norms help to explain how and why we have evolved as a cooperative species, but how do we ensure that no-one free rides on the generosity of others? This question is explored by behavioural economists who study a group of games known as *public good games*—an experimental vehicle for studying not only our tendencies to cooperate but also the role of social sanctions and punishments in sustaining cooperative behaviour. Public good games are developed from the economic concept of a public good.

In its purest form, a public good is something to which everyone has free and easy access—no-one is stopped from consuming the good and so it cannot easily be brought into private ownership. The classic example of a public good is a lighthouse—everyone sailing past a lighthouse can get the benefit of the light, but it is difficult to *charge* any single individual for the benefit of the light. So anyone wanting to make money out of a private business is unlikely to invest in a lighthouse because it would be difficult to make any money out of it. Some other motivation is needed to ensure that public goods such as lighthouses are provided. And economists have found that local communities are surprisingly good at ensuring that public goods are provided and maintained.

Behavioural economists have unravelled some of the factors that affect our behaviour towards public goods by using public goods games. In one such game, a group of experimental participants is gathered together and asked to make a contribution to a communal pot of money that will later be shared equally between the members of the group. This is a little like what a community would have to do if it wanted a pot of money to build a community park, for example. Many economists would predict that most people would make a contribution of nothing because they would reason that, regardless of whether or not they decided to contribute, the pot of money will be shared equally. So the best way for an individual to maximize her net gain is to have a share of the pot without also having to make a contribution herself. The problem with this reasoning is that if everyone thinks this way, and everyone plans to free-ride on the others' contributions, then there will be no money at all in the pot to share, and there will be no public goods. In this case, selfish individuals will create an outcome that is bad for the group as a whole.

Behavioural and experimental economists have found that, luckily, in public goods game experiments, people are surprisingly generous—in much the same way that people are generous in ultimatum games. Most participants will give quite a bit more than nothing. Variants of the public goods game experiments show that, when a third party observes others being mean in public goods experiments, then he is willing to pay to punish the uncooperative players—this phenomenon is known as *altruistic punishment*. People are prepared to forgo something themselves in order to punish others for violating social norms of generosity and cooperation. This is a form of cooperation in itself because altruistic punishment reinforces the cooperative behaviour of those who do give generously, and discourages the selfish behaviour of those who do not. Altruistic punishment in public goods games has been studied by neuroeconomists and neuroscientists. They find that experimental participants engaging in altruistic punishment experience neural activations in the brain's reward centres—this suggests that we feel pleasure when we punish others for violating social norms.

Altruistic punishment is an important phenomenon in the evolution of cooperation. In the modern world, altruistic punishment can help to explain why we are quick publicly to condemn socially unacceptable behaviour. Social media has made this much easier, with negative consequences too—for example, Twitter trolls. More generally these tendencies to cooperate and reinforce social norms can also explain why social information is such a powerful tool in manipulating behaviour. One example is the evidence on energy consumption—when energy consumers are told about the consumption of their neighbours, they are likely to adjust their own consumption towards the social reference point of friends' and neighbours' energy consumption. Similarly, when the UK's tax agency—Her Majesty's Revenue and Customs (HMRC)—wrote letters to late payers of tax bills containing some social information about others' behaviour and informing the recalcitrant that her behaviour was socially anomalous because most of her peers had paid their bills on time, this led to many (not all!) of the remaining late-payers paying up more quickly than a group of late payers who had received letters containing no reference to the social information about others' payment decisions.

Identity is another manifestation of our social natures and, in many ways, is like a very specific form of social signalling, similar in that sense to the role that image motivation plays in charitable giving, as discussed in Chapter 2. We identify with some groups more than others and this links back to social psychologist Henri Tajfel's early analysis of prejudice and discrimination. Tajfel wanted to understand why so many ordinary people were so in thrall to Hitler and the Nazi party. He focused on intergroup relations where we identify with a particular *in-group* and we are prepared to challenge and clash with *out-groups*, whom we see in some sense as our opposites. Tajfel also noted that it takes very little for a group of people to identify with each other and decide they want an ongoing relationship of mutual favourism. Simple preferences for particular types of art, even a simple coin toss, can separate one group from another. We are prepared to incur costs to identify ourselves with a particular group—for example, fans of pop stars such as Katy Perry will spend thousands of pounds or dollars in a year because they identify with other Katy Perry fans. Tajfel's insights about groups link into behavioural economists' analyses of identity. George Akerlof and Rachel Kranton have developed the analysis of identity—observing that what seem like perverse behaviours, including incurring self-harm in the form of tattoos and piercings, are an attempt to signal to our in-groups that we are with them.

Identity plays a particularly powerful role in politics. Most of us have a strong need to identify with others socially, politically, and culturally. In the aftermath of the UK's vote to leave the EU in June 2016, commentators observed that many who had voted 'Leave' were motivated by the sense that their identities had been lost or diluted by the growth of immigration from the EU. The irony is that, with a couple of notable exceptions (for example, Boston in Lincolnshire), the most ardent 'Leavers' among the general public, the ones who felt they had most to fear from immigrants, were living in areas with low immigration rates. Perhaps they were deciding that immigrants were an out-group on the basis of little direct experience at all, a phenomenon that would not have surprised Tajfel.

Herding and social learning

An important facet of our social natures is our tendency to imitate, herd, and follow the crowd. Sociologists explain herding as a reflection of two types of influence: *normative* and *informational*. Normative influences are the social norms that drive our decisions—many of us often want to fit in and do what others do. They may reflect evolved, instinctive responses. Many of our decisions, including economic and financial decisions, involve following other people, perhaps because we believe we can learn from them or perhaps because there is some more primitive instinctive process going on.

Social psychologist Solomon Asch found that, even in very simple decision-making tasks—for example, judging the relative length of lines—others can easily manipulate us. Asch found that when single, genuine experimental participants were included in groups of, say, nineteen experimental confederates all giving obviously wrong answers to very simple questions, the genuine experimental participants would often change their minds and switch from obviously correct answers to wrong ones, because that is what the group had decided. And this is not necessarily irrational behaviour, if the person is judging that it is not very likely that he is right and the nineteen others are wrong.

Fascinating new research into how and why we copy others is emerging, and one promising area for investigation for economists is the neuroeconomic analysis of *mirror neurons*. Mirror neurons are found in human and primate brains, and in some other animals too. Scientists believe that they may play a role when we imitate others. Neuroscientists have conducted experiments on monkeys using single neuron experiments, which involve monitoring firing rates from a single neuron. When a monkey moves in a certain way, the mirror neurons fire not only when the monkey under observation moves, but also when that monkey sees another monkey move. The fact that similar responses are seen in our primate ancestors may indicate that herding behaviour is automatic and 'hard-wired', and perhaps reflects our more primitive emotions including impulsiveness. It is possible that similar neural processes are generating our herding behaviour in economic and financial contexts too.

An important element in the economic analysis of herding builds on sociologists' insights about informational influence. Informational influence is about learning from others' actions. Where these actions are easily observable they can be a useful guide when alternative information is hard to find. Other people may know something we do not and so it might make sense to copy them—following the crowd may be a rational social learning device. However, sometimes following the crowd is just impulsive and we do it without thinking, perhaps reflecting evolved herding instincts.

There are very many examples in ordinary life. When I need some cash in a hurry and I see a long queue behind one ATM and no queue behind the next ATM, I save myself time by assuming that people are not using the second ATM for a reason—it is broken or the bank is charging an excessive fee. I learn from the group's decisions. This is neither wrong nor right—sometimes the herd has chosen the correct strategy, other times the herd has chosen the wrong strategy. Whether or not it is clever for me to follow the herd will depend on the circumstances. Other people's choices are also informative when we are choosing a restaurant. I would not usually go into an empty restaurant when the restaurant next door is crowded. I prefer the crowded restaurant even if I have to queue because the herd might know something I do not about the dodgy wine and food in the first restaurant, or the tasty food in the second. Is herding good or bad? It depends on whether those group judgements and decisions are right or wrong.

Herding also generates negative spillovers. If I am choosing between an empty restaurant and a crowded restaurant—why the crowded one? If I follow others into a crowded restaurant t. I am using social information about group decisions—but wha I have other, private information that is valuable but not directi observable by others? Imagine I have two pieces of information. one is a recommendation from a personal friend who has been visiting from Sydney and told me that the empty restaurant is the best undiscovered restaurant in London; the second is the information I can infer from observing other people's preferred choice of restaurant.

I may decide to follow the herd into the popular restaurant—and in ignoring my private information (my friend's recommendation) that information is now lost to anyone observing my behaviour. They would infer from my selection of restaurant that the empty restaurant does not have much to recommend it at all—they cannot see or know that I have private information suggesting the empty restaurant could, in fact, be very good. So they are likely to queue for the less good but crowded restaurant too, as are others following along behind them. In this way, social information about others' choices cascades through the herd. When herding leads to valuable private information being ignored because people are misled by the behaviour of the herd, it generates negative effects on others—a negative *herding externality*. The herd provides safety; and collective decision-making can, under certain assumptions, lead to better decisions. Collective information can be more accurate. But herding can also mean that valuable private information is ignored and lost.

Another reason to herd is because what others think of us matters to us. Our reputation is valuable and we try to guard it carefully, and this also links to the image motivation factors discussed in

Chapter 2. Our reputations often survive better if we are only wrong when others are wrong—to paraphrase economist John Maynard Keynes: reputations fare better if we are conventionally wrong than if we are unconventionally right. Rogue traders are an example of the vulnerability of a reputation built on contrarian choices. Spectacular gains can be made when a trader bids against financial market conventions. But when the crowd is right and the contrarian is wrong, her reputation cannot so easily be rescued if she cannot defend herself by saying: 'it was a common mistake'.

Evolution may well play a significant role because many other species share our social learning behaviour. The Adelie penguins of the Antarctic exhibit strong herding tendencies. They are in the middle of a food chain—they eat krill and are eaten by leopard seals. When finding food they face a dilemma—if they dive into the sea, they may find some krill to enjoy, or they may be attacked and eaten by a seal. Their best strategy is to employ some social learning and observe their fellow penguins before deciding what to do. The bravest and/or hungriest penguin will take a risk, and if the rest of the colony can see that no seal attacks him, then the others will follow—herding behind him into the sea. There are modern human parallels—we use consumer feedback and reviews to guide our purchases—made much easier with the growth of the Internet and online shopping. We are responsive to information about celebrities using particular products. All these ways in which we look to others when choosing what to buy reflect our susceptibility to social information.

Similarly, human herding is often about the security of being in a group. There is safety in numbers. Imagine crossing a busy road in Jakarta jammed with cars and motorbikes. The only way to get across that road is to move with a group of locals—learning from them the local pedestrians' habits, but also enjoying the safety and shelter of the crowds. A car is far more likely to run over a lone pedestrian than a crowd. There are corollaries in our civil lives:

class action suits rely on the fact that the crowd has more power and influence than single individuals, and it can protect us from injustice too—for example, if we group together to take legal action. An example is the Fen-Phen diet pills class action suit. The US Food and Drug Administration found that using Fen-Phen was associated with heart disease. More than 125,000 users of the diet pills filed a class action suit against the manufacturers, Wyeth, who eventually settled out of court at a cost of almost $16.6 million. Individuals who were powerless alone gathered together as a group to get justice for their collective.

Many of these are modern examples, but our herding instincts are old, deep-seated, and antediluvian. Our herding instincts are shared by many other species—for example, the penguins mentioned earlier. Herding is very much associated with animal behaviour. Cows' herding behaviour is an instinct that has evolved as a protection against predators. In humans as with many other animals, following others is an evolved survival strategy that enabled our ancestors to find food, shelter, and fertile mates. How do these deep-seated instincts play out in modern artificial environments in which internet and mobile technologies mediate our social relationships and interactions—when we buy and sell on eBay; and book our holidays and taxi cab rides using TripAdvisor, Airbnb, and Uber? Both the virtues and the vices of herding and social influence are magnified in our fast-moving computerized world. Financial crises today are driven by speculators chasing other speculators in search of profit, as they have done for centuries, from the time of Tulipmania (the 17th-century Dutch speculative euphoria around buying and selling tulip bulbs) and before.

Financial herding is a type of herding that has affected us all profoundly—either directly or indirectly. We live in a globalized, computerized, interdependent, financial system. The speed and magnitude of financial flows can be overwhelming— exemplified in the case of Navinder Singh Sarao, who was accused of contributing to Wall Street's 2010 trillion-dollar 'Flash Crash' by spoof trading from a computer in his parents' suburban London home. Herding has the power to destabilize markets and financial systems. It also has the power to disrupt our buying patterns, voting habits, religious views and practices, and cultural preferences. It can distort our social relationships and interactions.

Herding has wider implications too—in terms of welfare and well-being. Ethically, it could be problematic if business and government are using social information to manipulate decision-making, taking us towards a *1984*-style world of group-think and Big Brother. If there is commercial value in manipulating social decision-making then there are powerful incentives for business and government to invade individuals' privacy and mine personal information, leading to exploitation by modern hi-tech businesses. It can also affect our financial futures—for example, if group-think dominates pension fund trustees' decision-making processes, enabling mendacious individuals and groups to siphon off money, then large numbers of people will face a financially vulnerable old age. Unfortunately, pension fund fraud is not rare—and from Robert Maxwell onwards there have been many such stories—most recently in the UK are concerns about pension fund management for former employees of British Home Stores. The good news is that regulators are aware of these influences and are working on developing policies to limit the risks and ensure that pension funds are properly managed.

This chapter has explored the many ways in which social influences affect a wide range of our economic and financial decisions. We respond to social influences reflecting our perceptions of how we are doing relative to others, and how they are doing relative to us. Many people prefer to see more equal outcomes and do not like inequity, especially if it affects them personally. We trust and reciprocate, and many economic relationships depend on this social behaviour. We learn from others and we copy others. Many types of herding and social learning affect our economic and financial decisions. In all of this, behavioural economics brings together insights from social psychology, sociology, neuroscience, and evolutionary biology to explain how and why social influences have such a powerful pull on our economic and financial behaviour.

One interpretation of herding is that it is a quick decision-making tool—what behavioural economists call a *heuristic*—enabling us to economize on the time and cognitive effort of making all our decisions from scratch. For example, imagine you need to buy a new fridge, and you know that your neighbour has just spent a lot of time investigating the best brand of fridge to buy. Why would you repeat all that effort when you could just ask him for a recommendation? Your heuristic is to ask your neighbour—which will save you a lot of time and energy. But the problem with heuristics is that, while they are quick and convenient and often work well enough, they are associated with systematic behavioural biases. When we follow our neighbours and friends, we may be leveraging valuable social information, or we might just be repeating their mistakes. Furthermore, herding is only one type of heuristic—the behavioural economics literature on heuristics is vast, and in Chapter 4 we will cover some of the key insights.

Chapter 4
Quick thinking

Chapter 3 covered some of the ways in which our decisions are affected by social influences and the behaviour and attitudes of other people. Herding is a key example—we follow others because copying them is a quick way to decide what to do next. In many of our everyday choices we use these quick rules and this chapter explores some of the main heuristics and the consequences of using them, especially in terms of behavioural bias.

Traditionally, economists focus on the role of markets in coordinating the decisions and choices of many consumers and firms. In markets, prices play the pivotal role by signalling information about costs of production, and the balance of demand and supply. While markets serve a very important purpose, the price mechanism is fallible and all sorts of failures in markets mean that prices do not effectively capture all aspects of supply and demand. Economists know this better than anyone and many economists spend their lives analysing how and why markets fail—mostly focusing on market and institutional failures.

Behavioural economists bring in an additional dimension, not by looking at markets and their supporting institutions such as governments and legal systems, but by examining the behaviour of the individual decision-makers that constitute a market. In this, behavioural economists move away from the standard economic assumptions—that people use relatively complex and mathematical decision-making rules when deciding what to do, what to buy, what to sell, and how hard to work.

Traditionally, economists assume that, while markets fail, the people using markets are super-rational beings. Sometimes these super-rational beings make decisions that, with the benefit of hindsight and better information, they could improve. But, on the basis of the information available at the time, they do their best and they do not repeat their mistakes. These rational agents' choices are a stable reflection of their underlying preferences—for example, if a rational being prefers books to chocolate, and prefers chocolate to shoes, then they will also prefer books to shoes. Their preferences are stable and consistent. They process all the most up-to-date information they have and use mathematical reasoning to figure out from that the best, most optimal solution. There is plenty of economic analysis addressing what happens when this information is unreliable or imperfect in some way, but most economists do not focus on other, less mathematical ways of choosing and deciding. This is where behavioural economics comes in—with a softer view of rationality.

For behavioural economists, the problem with traditional economics is that these assumptions about people's decision-making tools are incomplete and/or unrealistic. In reality, we make many of our everyday decisions quickly, without too much thought at all. This is not stupid or irrational—quite the opposite. We would be more stupid and irrational to spend hours collecting information and carefully calculating a strategy for some of the everyday decisions that have just a fleeting impact on our lives. Sometimes we want or need to decide quickly. That does not mean that thinking quickly is a good thing either. When we decide too quickly, we make mistakes. When we reflect back over the day we might decide that, if we had taken more time deciding, we might have made better choices. This chapter explores some of these themes, ocusing on the quick thinking rules and associated mistakes that we make in our everyday decision-making.

Quick decisions using heuristics

Deciding quickly is difficult when we are overwhelmed by information: when we face *information overload*. It is also difficult to decide quickly and accurately when we are overwhelmed by choices: when we are facing *choice overload*. Traditionally economists have assumed that choice is a good thing and that having more choices is better than having fewer choices. Many choices mean that each of us can more easily find products and services that neatly match our needs and desires, thus boosting our welfare. In the real world however, having a very wide range of choices available does not seem to improve outcomes.

Choice experts Sheena Iyengar and Mark Lepper explored how and why choice can demotivate shoppers and students. In one set of experiments, they asked shoppers in a grocery store to browse stalls selling jams: one stall had twenty-four varieties of jam on offer; the other displayed just five. While shoppers spent more time browsing the stall with lots of jams on offer, they bought more from the stall with the smaller range. Perhaps the shoppers were so overwhelmed and demotivated by the range of choices available, their ability to make any choice at all was impaired. In another choice experiment, two groups of students were set different assessment tasks. Students in one group were instructed to choose one essay topic from a list of thirty. Students in the other group were instructed to choose one essay from a list of six. Like the shopping scenario, performance and motivation was better for the students facing more limited choices. The students offered the more limited set of choices wrote longer and better essays.

In the modern world, the problem of choice overload is particularly profound and is exacerbated by information overload too. When facing choice overload, consumers decide quickly; for example, they may choose one of the first items on a list rather than fully considering all the options offered to them. If choices are too complex, and especially if they relate to 'boring' decisions that have no tangible and immediate benefits (e.g. choosing a pension plan), we might just abandon our attempt to choose anything at all. Subsequent evidence about choice overload has been mixed but a recent study from Alexander Chernev and colleagues has shown that context is important: the complexity of choices offered, the difficulty of tasks, participants' uncertainty about their preferences, and their desires to minimize effort—all are associated with increased susceptibility to choice overload.

Paralleling the wide range of choices we face in buying everything from jam and bread through to complex financial products, there is a large volume of complex information, both online and offline, which is not necessarily quick and easy to navigate. In contrast to the standard view from economics, behavioural economists are discovering that more information is not necessarily better. In many everyday situations, we do not want to waste time and energy with complex calculations and instead we use simple rules of thumb to help us to decide quickly. Behavioural economists call these simple decision rules *heuristics*. Sometimes heuristics work well, but not always. Other times they lead us into errors and mistakes.

It is often sensible to use heuristics. Only a foolish person would spend days exploring all the different online and offline sales outlets before deciding to buy a particular type of car, TV, fridge, or phone, just in the hope of saving a few pounds. For smaller, everyday choices this is particularly true. I do not conduct a comprehensive research exercise each time I buy a loaf of bread. I do not waste time comparing prices of bread across all London supermarkets because, while I might save 50 pence on the bread, I would have to spend £5 travelling to the cheapest supermarket, as well as having to factor in the value of the time I had wasted.

This insight is consistent with standard economic analyses of the costs of transacting. Most economists would agree that we economize not only when deciding what to buy but also in the process of trading, bargaining, and collecting information.

Behavioural economists take the insight further, however, in arguing that we are not making calculations about these transaction costs either. We use heuristics and these stop us wasting time thinking about *any* of the direct and indirect costs of our different options too deeply at all. Going back to my choice of bread—I might use a range of heuristics. I might buy the same brand I bought last time because I remember it was tasty. If I am trying to be healthy, I might pick a brand with packaging that represents healthiness—more paper, less plastic perhaps, illustrated with imagery of green plants and seeds. If I am at home and feeling lazy, I will just go around the corner to my local convenience store, even though I know that their prices are significantly higher than those of the big supermarkets. But these processes will operate almost unconsciously. I will not consider the information offered by the bread bakers and suppliers with any sort of analytical depth, and I will not think too deeply about the relative transaction costs of the different options either.

The problem with using heuristics is that, often, they lead us into mistakes and bias. Psychologists Daniel Kahneman and Amos Tversky were pioneers in analysing heuristics and this work has been popularized in Kahneman's 2011 book—*Thinking, Fast and Slow*. Using a range of experiments and insights, Kahneman and Tversky showed how a small set of heuristics lead us into making systematic, predictable mistakes. When we decide quickly, sometimes our choices are distorted away from what is best for us.

Kahneman and Tversky explore three main types of heuristics and the behavioural biases associated with them: availability, representativeness, and anchoring/adjustment.

Using available information

When we are making a decision, particularly if we are in a hurry, we do not reflect carefully on all the information we have. Instead, we will use information that is easy to access, retrieve, and recall. Using our knowledge is like rifling through a filing cabinet when we are in a hurry to get to a meeting. We tend to go to the first folder we can find that has any relevance, but we do not have the time and energy to go through every folder carefully looking for the most relevant information. Sometimes this means that we miss important information and make mistakes.

When we rely on easily retrievable information instead of looking fully and carefully at all relevant information—Kahneman and Tversky call this the *availability heuristic*. Availability also links with concepts from psychology: *primacy* and *recency effects*. We remember more easily the first and last bits of information we come across, and information in the middle is much more easily forgotten.

The availability heuristic can explain our habitual behaviours. My husband and I enjoy travelling, and I usually book the flights and hotels. I am aware that there is a large, complex range of travel agencies online and offline, but I tend to use the same one each time because I can easily remember how to use it. I remember how good (or bad) my last experience was—and the online sites help me with that by allowing me to store information about my past experiences. Frequent email reminders from the online providers reinforce these memories. I might be missing out on all sorts of bargains because I do not shop around enough. I do not want to be a sucker so I do occasionally take a look around on other sites, but usually the prices for hotels and flights are not that different—whether this reflects collusive over-charging by the travel agents, competitive price pressure, or a combination of both, I do not know. Either way, when I think about it carefully,

Quick thinking

I feel reassured that my speedy use of readily retrievable information is not leading me into big, important mistakes, though I may be wrong.

Sometimes we use the availability heuristic more consciously (e.g. when we are choosing our passwords) and this increases our vulnerability to cyber privacy and security violations by hackers, spammers, and phishers. A good password is hard to remember. We might use the availability heuristic to devise memorable passwords for ourselves—but a password that is easy to remember is also easy to crack. Security firm SplashData compiles an annual list of the worst passwords. The commonest and most enduring password is '123456' (it has made the top of SplashData's list for a few years running). The second most common is 'password'. Both are easily retrievable using the availability heuristic, but it would be well-known to any hacker that these passwords are commonly used.

Policy-makers and competition regulators are interested in how we use heuristics, especially in the context of consumers' 'switching' behaviour—we are slow to switch our energy, mobile phone, and financial services suppliers, even when we could get a better deal elsewhere. Why not switch to better deals more often? Perhaps it is laziness and procrastination—but it might also be the availability heuristic at work. Unless we have had a memorably bad experience, we tend to stick with what we know, because we know what we know. Policy-makers are increasingly concerned that businesses can exploit consumers' inertia. When businesses are not disciplined by competitive pressure from consumers (i.e. consumers deciding to go for a better bargain elsewhere), then businesses have no incentive to improve the deals they offer. What is the solution? Price comparison sites are one way to help us access better information more quickly. Governments are also working on ways to make it easier for us to switch suppliers, as will be explored in more detail in Chapter 9—'Economic behaviour and public policy'.

Using representations

Another of Tversky and Kahneman's heuristics that leads us into bias is the *representativeness heuristic*. We often decide by analogy—we draw, sometimes spurious, comparisons with other superficially similar events. Behavioural economists and psychologists have used a wide range of experiments to show how we jump too quickly to the conclusion that scenarios are similar. We also fit our perceptions of others with our pre-existing stereotypes.

Tversky and Kahneman illustrate the representativeness heuristic with a range of experiments. In one, they ask their experimental participants to judge a person's likely profession. Some people were given a description of Steve. They were told that Steve is shy and withdrawn and has an eye for detail. Given this information, participants were more likely to predict that Steve is a librarian, even when the objective information about the relative likelihood that he is a librarian does not support their judgement.

Tversky and Kahneman capture a similar phenomenon in their experiments exploring 'the Linda problem'. They asked another group of experimental participants to read some information about a woman named Linda. The participants were told that Linda is in her 30s. She is clever, single, and outspoken. She is concerned about social justice and discrimination, and has been an anti-nuclear protestor. Then the experimental participants are asked:

'Which is more probable?

1. Linda is a bank teller
2. Linda is a bank teller and is active in the feminist movement.'

Many people select option 2: that Linda is a bank teller active in the feminist movement, even though this category is a sub-set of

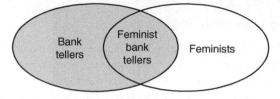

1. The Linda problem—a conjunction fallacy.

option 1—(all) bank tellers. At most, option 2 is as probable as option 1. It cannot be more probable. This mistake is called the *conjunction fallacy*: it is about the probability of what theorists call 'conjoint events'—events occurring together, as illustrated in Figure 1.

The conjunction of the two events—first, that Linda is a bank teller and, second, that she is also a feminist, is judged by many people to be more likely than just a single event—that Linda is a bank teller, even though Linda as a bank teller covers a larger set of possibilities—all bank tellers, feminist or not. Given that there is some chance that Linda is not a feminist given the information presented, then, if people are properly applying the rules of probability, they should decide that option 1 is more likely.

Why do so many people ignore simple rules of probability? The idea is that we do not make our decisions purely on the basis of mathematical, statistical rules. Instead, we form narrative accounts in our mind. Stories have a powerful pull on our imaginations. Employing the representativeness heuristic, we match our judgements with our knowledge of prior scenarios and stereotypes. Linda's story makes us think she is more likely to be a feminist and so we choose the option that explicitly includes the possibility that she is a feminist. Even if we know the rules of statistics and probability, this knowledge of probability rules does not seem relevant to us and we discard it in favour of a coherent narrative—a story that seems to capture who Linda is and what she does.

The representativeness heuristic can also distort our judgement if we are slow to adjust our prior beliefs to new information, and this links to the problems of *confirmation bias* and *cognitive dissonance*.

Confirmation bias occurs when we anchor our judgement rigidly to our prior beliefs. This is a common phenomenon in political debates and in disputes between the Left and Right. In his 2014 book, *Demonizing the President: The Foreignization of Barak Obama*, Martin Parlett explores reactions to Barak Obama's role in the killing of Osama bin Laden in April 2011. On the surface, it might be hard to imagine that Barak Obama's role in bin Laden's killing could be interpreted as a pro-terrorism action, however the conservative newspaper *The Washington Times* suggested that Obama had honoured bin Laden by allowing him full traditional Muslim burial rites. The conservative view was that Obama is a terrorist sympathizer, and so any of Obama's actions, even the killing of a terrorist leader, was interpreted from a conservative perspective as pro-terrorist.

In the UK in 2015, the surprise election of Jeremy Corbyn as the Labour Party's Leader of the Opposition also illustrates confirmation bias. On his first outing at Prime Minister's Questions he included questions from voters when usually the questions are formulated by the UK Members of Parliament, with the Leader of the Opposition taking the lead. His supporters interpreted this as an excellent illustration of his laudable democratic inclinations; his detractors interpreted it as evidence that he did not know what he was doing and could not think of any questions of his own. In either case, Jeremy Corbyn's actions mostly did not change people's opinions of him; his actions just confirmed what they already believed.

While confirmation bias is about interpreting new evidence in the light of our existing beliefs, *cognitive dissonance* is about conflicts between our beliefs and our actions. We may believe ourselves to be good, charitable people and yet regularly walk past homeless people asking for money. Our actions conflict with our belief about ourselves and so we rationalize our actions. We might decide that the homeless person should be selling the *Big Issue*—we would buy a magazine from them if they were selling one. Or we might conclude that the homeless person is a con artist who really just wants to steal our wallet. Or we might decide that giving them money will not help them really because they would just spend it on drugs. In any of these cases, we have manipulated our perception of a situation so that our prior beliefs, in this case about our capacity for generosity, remain unchallenged.

George Akerlof and William Dickens confirmed this tendency with some behavioural experiments. They asked students to insult each other, for example by telling them: 'you are shallow, untrustworthy, and dull'. Akerlof and Dickens found that the students delivering the insults adjusted their attitudes towards their targets by becoming more genuinely critical of the victims of their insults. The students delivering the insults did not want to challenge their own belief in themselves as a 'nice' person, and the only way to reconcile this dissonance was to adjust their beliefs about others. Akerlof and Dickens conclude that the students' responses may parallel the ways in which people justify violent and aggressive behaviour more generally.

Anchoring and adjustment

The third sort of bias occurs when we anchor our decisions around a reference point, and adjust our choices relative to this reference point. Again, Tversky and Kahneman use a range of experimental evidence to illustrate the idea. In one study, they asked school children to make quick guesses about arithmetic tasks. One group of children were asked to estimate 8 x 7 x 6 x 5 x 4 x 3 x 2 x 1. A second group of children was asked to estimate 1 x 2 x 3 x 4 x 5 x 6 x 7 x 8. The guesses should have been similar but the children who were asked to start with 8 x 7 x... came up with higher estimates than the children asked to calculate 1 x 2 x.... One explanation for this is that the first group of children were anchoring their estimates around the first number they saw—'8' and getting a higher answer than the second group, who were anchoring their estimates around the '1'. The children's answers illustrate the more general problem we get when we adjust around an initial anchor—insufficient adjustment. Our decisions and choices are distorted by our starting position.

One everyday example of anchoring and adjustment can be illustrated using the Sydney housing market. In Australia, many houses are sold via auction and this gives academics a rich database to study. Auction clearance rates are an important signal about the buoyancy of the Sydney housing market, and 2015 was a bumper year with house prices growing, on average in Sydney, by around 20 per cent. This bubble burst (temporarily) in late 2015, and auction clearance rates plummeted from rates of up to 90 per cent (i.e. 90 per cent of the houses listed for auction were successfully sold) down to under 50 per cent (see <www.abs.gov.au/ausstats/abs@.nsf/mf/6416.0>). By early 2016 potential home-sellers had responded to this downturn and auction clearance rates were going up again, but only because the number of sellers putting their houses up for auction had fallen so fast—the number of houses listed for auction fell from hundreds in late 2015 to just a handful by early 2016. One possible explanation could be that potential sellers had anchored their expectations to a particular sale price. Once they saw that they were not likely to achieve this price, they decided not to sell rather than just allowing market forces to determine the outcome for them.

In some senses, the anchoring element of anchoring and adjustment heuristics overlaps with the availability heuristic described earlier. Our reference points are often more cognitively accessible than other information. For example, often we use the status quo as the reference point—we tend to avoid change away from the existing situation. Sometimes this leads to *status quo bias* and *familiarity bias*—people are resistant to change, or they judge events according to how different they are to the current situation. In our everyday lives, many of our judgements are based around how much our decisions will move us away from the status quo. When we are looking for a new job, or selling a house, our perception of a fair wage or a fair house price will be based around what we are earning today, or the price we paid for our house when we bought it, or how much our neighbour got when she sold hers. The problem is that these judgements may have very little to do with market forces of supply and demand. These judgements may also stop markets working smoothly.

Businesses and policy-makers can exploit our status quo bias in manipulating our decision-making—for example, by setting the status quo through default options. The default options we are offered represent the status quo, and we have to make a conscious effort to change away from these defaults. Businesses often cynically exploit this tendency by designing complex default options to confuse us—as Figure 2 implies.

However, status quo bias and default options can be used in more constructive ways by policy-makers—to solve the problems that can emerge from our inertia. One key example relates to pensions. Finding the money to pay for people's retirements, given ageing populations and lengthening life expectancies, is a serious and growing policy problem for many advanced economies. Behavioural economists Shlomo Benartzi and Richard Thaler devised a pensions scheme based around the status quo bias and the related idea that people tend to stick with default options, where the default represents the status quo. Their scheme, which they called 'Save More Tomorrow' (SMarT), was designed so that a proportion of future pay rises goes into workers' pension pots. So, unless a worker opts out, when they get a pay rise, part of it will go into their SMarT pension fund. This scheme also means that workers do not feel that they are losing anything relative to their current pay because only salary *increases* are taken into the

2. Confusing default options.

SMarT fund. And the workers still have a choice. Automatically contributing a proportion of any salary increases is the default option, but if a worker does not want to lose any of their pay rise into their pension fund, then they can opt out. Benartzi and Thaler found that pension contributions increased significantly just by manipulating default options in this way—an insight that has led to the redesign of pension schemes and policies in a number of countries.

Since Kahneman and Tversky's pioneering studies in the 1970s, the range of heuristics and biases identified by economists and psychologists has grown rapidly. The Wikipedia entry for 'cognitive bias' currently lists well over a hundred different types of bias. Developing an analytical structure to these insights would help us to understand more deeply how and why these biases affect our choices. Many behavioural economists have been working on this—to develop theories to capture the key insights. One of the most influential theoretical developments in this field is *prospect theory*. In constructing this theory, Kahneman and Tversky developed their early ideas about heuristics and bias into a richer and more systematic analysis of decision-making, applied in particular to how we decide in risky situations. We will explore prospect theory, and some other competing theories about risky decisions, in Chapter 5.

Chapter 5
Risky choices

In Chapter 4, we explored a range of ways in which our quick
decisions can lead us into making mistakes, and this is particularly
true when we are facing risk and uncertainty. When we decide to
cross the road, buy a lottery ticket, invest our money, or take out
a payday loan, all these decisions involve risk and uncertainty.
Economists usually think of risk as quantifiable—if we can just
figure out that the chance that we will get hit by a bus when
crossing the road is, say, 1 in 8,000, then we can decide whether
or not we want to take that risk, depending on how we value
the consequences.

Economists also usually assume that we decide between risky
options according to how much we like taking risks, or not. Our
risk preferences do not change just because one of the options we
are facing is presented and framed in a different way. If I buy a
lottery ticket, my chance of winning £1 million is 1 in 14 million—so
I am not likely to win, but I balance these low odds against the
prospect of a very large prize, and decide according to my risk
preference. Do I like taking risks? Or do I prefer to avoid risks if
I can? Or perhaps I am risk neutral and do not mind too much
either way? If I prefer to avoid risk, I will not buy the ticket; if
I like taking risks, I will.

Behavioural economists challenge this understanding of risk. They focus on the way our perceptions of risks shift in different situations. One example is the way we judge risks depending on how easily we remember information, and this links to the availability heuristic, explored in Chapter 4. We choose, not on the basis of all the information we can find, but just on the basis of information that is quickly available to us—information we can recall or retrieve quickly and easily. Newspaper headlines about plane crashes are an example: we read about plane crashes regularly and these stories are often accompanied by very memorable, vivid, and emotive images of wreckages and distraught relatives. This leads us into a misperception that airplane crashes are a lot more likely than pedestrian fatalities. We are more likely to be killed crossing the road, but pedestrian fatalities rarely get beyond the local newspapers. We may take a lot more care and worry a lot more when we are deciding to fly, when really we should be taking more care when we are crossing the road.

Another mistake we make when making risky decisions is we inflate the impact of losses relative to gains. Many behavioural experiments have shown that people suffer more from a loss than they gain pleasure from an equivalent gain—for example, we tend to care a lot more about losing £10 than we do about winning £10. This phenomenon is called *loss aversion*—and it has been found to apply to a wide range of people's decisions.

One example affects housing markets: when homeowners see house prices falling, they are reluctant to sell because, by selling, they probably would have to experience a loss from the lower house prices. So homeowners postpone their selling decisions, until, suddenly, many more homeowners are forced to sell simultaneously—perhaps because economic conditions have deteriorated or mortgage interest rates have risen. The housing market gets flooded with properties for sale, and ironically, homeowners' losses are then likely to be magnified, all because loss aversion delayed people's decisions to sell sooner.

Behavioural economists are developing theories that capture some of the human, psychological aspects of risk-taking—to compete with the standard economics assumption that people carefully, consistently, and mathematically balance information about risks.

Prospect theory versus expected utility theory

The key model of risk in behavioural economics was developed by Daniel Kahneman and Amos Tversky, and, to some extent, it formalizes some of the key concepts from their analyses of heuristics and bias explored in Chapter 4. Prospect theory is about future risky prospects: when we buy a house, for example, we may have two prospects available to us. Imagine a first-time buyer who is not sure whether to buy a flat, in a convenient but expensive urban location; or a larger house in a less convenient but cheaper suburban or rural location. Another person might be balancing two employment prospects. Imagine a young graduate who faces two prospects: she can choose an unpaid internship that might lead to a much more interesting and/or more highly paid job in the future; or she can choose a steady, quite well-paid job which will earn her a steady income. Every day we are balancing different risky prospects against each other.

As a starting point in the development of prospect theory, Kahneman and Tversky critique some of the key elements of the standard economic approach to risk: *expected utility theory*. What is expected utility theory? 'Utility' is the word economists use to denote happiness and satisfaction, and expected utility theory explores how we decide about different options depending on what we expect the options to deliver in the future—in terms of our future utility. But we are not perfect forecasters and sometimes these expectations may turn out to be wrong.

Expected utility theory is founded on a range of restrictive assumptions about behaviour. Expected utility theorists assume that people make full use of all relevant, available information.

They also assume that we use relatively complex mathematical tools to ensure that we are maximizing our utility—they assume that we are doing the very best we can possibly do, and so we are choosing the options that give us the highest level of expected happiness and satisfaction that we could hope to achieve, given the information we have when we decide. Once we have identified this best choice, we do not change our minds. Our choices are not inconsistent. If we prefer apples to oranges, and oranges to bananas, then we will also prefer apples to bananas.

Behavioural paradoxes

According to Kahneman and Tversky, the problem with expected utility theory is that it cannot easily explain some common behavioural paradoxes, including (amongst others) the Allais Paradox and the Ellsberg Paradox.

Maurice Allais, the 19th-century French economist, showed how people's choices in risky situations are often inconsistent and one famous behavioural paradox—the *Allais Paradox*—is named in his honour. It shows that people do not have a stable, steady response to different risky outcomes. Specifically, if someone is given the option of a certain outcome alongside a series of risky options, then they will prefer the certain outcome even if, with a different set of prospects, they would be prepared to take risks. Kahneman and Tversky called this effect the *certainty effect*, and confirmed its existence with their own experiments. They wanted to see if people were prepared to take a small additional risk in order to increase their payoffs by—say $1. If people have consistent preferences for risk-taking, then a risk-loving person would take the risk and a risk-averse person would not. Kahneman and Tversky tested for the Allais Paradox by including an option that was guaranteed with certainty so they could see if this distorted people's choices, especially the choices of those who were usually more inclined towards risk-taking.

Table 1 Allais Paradox games

	Choose one option	
	Game 1	**Game 2**
Option 1	$24 with certainty	34% chance of $24
		66% chance of £0
Option 2	1% chance of $0	33% chance of $25
	33% chance of $25	67% chance of $0
	66% chance of $24	

Kahneman and Tversky's experimental participants were asked to assess different sets of prospects across two games: Game 1 and Game 2. If you were one of their participants you would have been asked to choose one of two options for each game. For Game 1 you have two options. You can either have $24 guaranteed with certainty (i.e. a 100 per cent chance you will get $24) or you can take a gamble giving you a slightly higher, 1 per cent, chance of nothing but the possibility of winning more than $24—including a 33 per cent chance of $25 and a 66 per cent chance of $24, with an overall 99 per cent chance at winning at least $24. These options are summarized in Table 1.

On its own, the set of prospects from Game 1 cannot reveal anything. A risk-averse person might select Option 1 because it offered $24 with certainty. A risk-seeking gambler might decide to take a chance on an additional $1 from winning a $25 payoff by selecting the second option, even though it increases his chances of $0 by a small amount. Either person's choice would be consistent with expected utility theory. But we can see if there are *inconsistencies* by comparing the players' choices with those from Game 2, which includes a second set of options—also summarized in Table 1.

The key difference between Game 1 and Game 2 is that Game 2 does not offer any certain outcome: the first option is a 34 per cent chance of $24 and a 66 per cent chance of $0. As for Game 1, the second option offers a slightly lower chance to win a little more—a 33 per cent chance of $25, but also a slightly higher chance of nothing at all—a 67 per cent chance of $0. So Game 2 is similar in many ways to Game 1 *except* it does not include any certain option.

Expected utility theory predicts that the outcome will be determined by a person's risk preferences, and there will be a trade-off between risk and rewards. If there are two types of people—a risk-averse, cautious person and a risk-loving gambler—the cautious person will always take the safe option, the gambler will always take the risky option. For Game 1 the gambler will take an extra chance in the hope of getting $25—they will trade the slightly higher risk of nothing for the slightly higher reward. For Game 2, they will also take a chance on $25—in both cases they would choose Option 2 because they like taking risks.

The cautious person should be the opposite—in both cases they would choose Option 1 because, for both Game 1 and Game 2, this is the safe option associated with smaller chances of getting nothing at all. For Game 1, choosing Option 1 means no chance of getting zero. For Game 2, the risk of zero is lower with Option 1 at 66 per cent, than for Option 2, when the chance of zero is slightly higher at 67 per cent.

How do real people play this game? Confirming previous experimental studies, Kahneman and Tversky found that people's choices are not consistent: gamblers are not always risk-takers. Many people will select Option 1 (the certain, safe option) from Game 1, but Option 2 (the more risky option) from Game 2. Kahneman and Tversky interpreted this evidence as confirming the existence of the certainty effect. Many people will be happy to take a chance and gamble, but when they are offered a certain outcome this distorts their choices away from taking additional risks for higher rewards.

How does this link into everyday choices? Perhaps it affects how we play for prizes in competitions. Kahneman and Tversky also designed a holiday games version of the certainty effect games. In one game, participants were asked to choose between an option for a 50 per cent chance of a three-week tour of England, France, and Italy versus a certain (100 per cent guaranteed) outcome of a one-week tour of England. Notice that the chances of the lesser English holiday are twice as good as the chances of the better European holiday. Most (78 out of 100 participants) chose the lesser but certain option—the guaranteed one-week tour of England.

In a second game, however, participants were prepared to take more risks when playing for holiday prizes. The relative probabilities were the same as for the first game—the English holiday was twice as likely as the European holiday—but no certain, 100 per cent option was included. The prospects were a 5 per cent chance of a three-week European holiday and a 10 per cent chance at the one-week English holiday. When offered the 5 per cent chance at the European holiday, 67 out of 100 participants took that option in preference to the better chance of the holiday in England. Even though the relative balance of probabilities was the same, participants had swapped their preferences from the more probable (in fact certain) but lesser prize, to the better but more unlikely prize. So the certainty effect appeared to be driving participants' decisions in the holiday games too. Kahneman and Tversky attributed this to *weighting*: we do not weight all probabilities equally, and tend to give certain outcomes more weight than less certain outcomes. Certainty distracts us.

Another famous behavioural paradox described by Kahneman and Tversky is the *Ellsberg Paradox*, named after the economist and military analyst Daniel Ellsberg, once employed by the RAND Corporation. He was also perhaps an early role model for modern day whistle-blowers and journalists including Edward Snowden and Julian Assange: Ellsberg released the 'Pentagon Papers',

Table 2 Ellsberg Paradox games

| | Which would you bet on? | |
	Game 1	**Game 2**
Option 1	Red	Red or yellow
Option 2	Black	Black or yellow

documenting the US government's controversial decisions during the Vietnam War for the *New York Times* in 1971.

Ellsberg's PhD research was a study of risky decisions and in one of his experiments, he told his experimental participants that he had filled an urn with ninety balls: thirty of which were red and sixty of which were either black or yellow, but the experimental participants were not given precise information about how many of the sixty balls were black and how many were yellow. Ellsberg then asked his experimental participants to choose which option they would select if they were asked to take a bet on the colour of a ball to be drawn at random from the urn. The options for this set of games are set out in Table 2.

Notice that both sets of options are essentially similar. For Game 1, Option 1 is to choose 'red'; Option 2 is to choose 'black'. For Game 2, the options are the same as for the Game 1 choices, except that 'or yellow' has been added in the same way to both options. Expected utility theorists might predict that if someone chooses Option 1 (red) for Game 1, they would also choose Option 1 (red or yellow) from Game 2 because the chances of drawing a red ball are not going to change from Game 1 to Game 2. Similarly, their choices will be consistent if they choose Option 2 (black) from Game 1 and Option 2 (black or yellow) from Game 2.

One interpretation is that people can calculate exactly the chances of 'red' and 'black or yellow' because they have been given the information they need to calculate this beforehand. But given the prior information, they have no exact information about the separate chances of picking a black or yellow ball (they just know the overall chances of black or yellow). So for Game 1, Option 2 is ambiguous; and for Game 2, Option 1 is ambiguous. Most people avoid the ambiguous option—they experience *ambiguity aversion*. We are not being at all irrational when we avoid ambiguous outcomes, but Kahneman and Tversky argue that ambiguity aversion is not easy to explain using expected utility theory, and they aimed to develop their prospect theory so that it *was* consistent with ambiguity aversion.

Inconsistent choices

In developing prospect theory, Kahneman and Tversky were keen to develop an alternative to expected utility theory which could incorporate the anomalous behaviour identified in the Allais and Ellsberg experiments, and also some additional effects that Kahneman and Tversky had noted in their own experiments.

What are these effects? Kahneman and Tversky also found that people were prepared to take on more risk if they were trying to avoid losses, and less risk when gambling for gains. Kahneman and Tversky argued that preference for taking risks when facing losses is the mirror image of the preference for taking risks in the context of gains—and so they called this effect the *reflection effect*.

Kahneman and Tversky demonstrated the reflection effect with the set of games shown in Table 3.

The payoffs for these two games are similar. In both games, participants choose between a risky option (Option 1) and a certain outcome (Option 2). The only difference is that Game 1 involves a gain and Game 2 involves a loss. Expected utility theorists would predict that a risk-seeking player would choose

Table 3 Reflection effect games

| | **Which would you choose?** | |
	Game 1	Game 2
Option 1	An 80% chance of winning $4,000, and a 20% chance of winning $0	An 80% chance of losing $4,000, and a 20% chance of losing $0
Option 2	A certain payoff of $3,000	A certain loss of $3,000

Option 1 in both cases, and a risk-averse player would choose Option 2 in both cases, but Kahneman and Tversky found that people's behaviour did not follow the pattern predicted by expected utility theory. Most participants (80 out of 100) chose the certain outcome for Game 1, but most (92 out of 100) chose the risky option for Game 2. They were prepared to take risks to avoid a loss, but preferred the certain outcome when offered prospects of gains. With this evidence Kahneman and Tversky confirmed the existence of a reflection effect—people are willing to take on more risks to avoid losses.

Kahneman and Tversky suggested that this could explain why people prefer *contingent insurance* (i.e. insurance payouts contingent on specific events such as fire, damage, or theft) versus *probabilistic insurance* (i.e. policies in which there is no guaranteed cover and payouts are determined by chance).

A probabilistic insurance deal could incorporate a reduction of regular insurance premiums by half for the insurance policy-holder if, in return, they were prepared to take some chance that they would bear all costs themselves. Then, if there is loss or damage, a toss of a coin will determine what happens next—either a 50 per cent chance that the policy-holder pays the remaining half of the premium and the insurance company covers all the costs of losses, or a 50 per cent chance that the policy-holder covers all the costs of the losses themselves and the insurance company returns their premium payments. Kahneman and Tversky argue that, in essence, the purchase of a burglar alarm is similar—people pay for a reduced risk of loss, not for eliminating the loss entirely, yet when offered probabilistic insurance most people avoid it. If they were consistent in their risk preferences, a risk-seeking person might prefer probabilistic insurance.

Kahneman and Tversky also identified a third effect—the *isolation effect*. This is about when we ignore important elements in the alternatives we face. We isolate specific bits of information, rather than looking at all the relevant information in its entirety. Kahneman and Tversky set out their findings from another set of experimental games to illustrate the isolation effect. One of the games includes options involving a sequence of possibilities, as shown in Table 4.

These games are set up carefully so that the payoffs the players could expect from both games are identical. To show this we need to think about the chances of the different range of options.

Table 4 Isolation effect games

	Game 1: a sequential game	Game 2: a one-stage game
	Stage 1: you have a 25% chance of moving to Stage 2 (and a 75% chance of not moving to Stage 2). If you were to move to Stage 2, which option would you choose?	**Choose one option**
Option 1	An 80% chance of winning $4,000, and a 20% chance of winning $0	A 20% of winning $4,000, and a 80% chance of winning $0
Option 2	A certain payoff of $3,000	A 25% chance of winning $3,000, and a 75% chance of winning $0

For Game 1, players have only a 25 per cent chance of moving to Stage 2—so there is a 75 per cent chance they will win nothing at all because this is the likelihood that they will not even get to Stage 2. When calculating their payoffs, participants should allow for this fact—that they only have a 25 per cent of getting to a stage when they will actually win anything at all.

So—for Game 1, Option 1, the *expected value* of the different options will be 25 per cent (the chance of moving to Stage 2) multiplied by an 80 per cent chance at $4,000 and a 20 per cent chance of nothing:

25 per cent x {(80% x $4,000) + (20% x $0)} = $800

For Game 1, Option 2, given the 25 per cent chance of getting to the second stage, when the player is guaranteed $3,000, the expected value will be 25 per cent x 100 per cent x $3,000:

25 per cent x {100% x $3,000} = $750

For Game 2, Kahneman and Tversky constructed the expected value of the options to be identical to those in Game 1 but there is no first stage—the players go straight to two options outlined and it is easier to calculate the payoffs because even the cleverest mathematicians need only to think about a single set of options:

Option 1:
= 20 per cent x $4,000 = $800
Option 2:
= 25 per cent x $3,000 = $750

Notice that, just in terms of the expected value of the options, these games are identical. The expected value from Option 1, in both games, is $800. The expected value from Option 2, in both games, is $750. So we can make some comparisons. If expected utility theory is correct, a person choosing Option 2 from Game 1 should choose Option 2 from Game 2 too. Yet Kahneman and Tversky found that a majority of their participants (78 out of 100) chose Option 2 from Game 1, but a majority (65 out of 100) chose Option 1 from Game 2. Kahneman and Tversky suggest that perhaps people were forgetting about the first stage of the game in Game 1. They were forgetting that, to start with, they had only had a 25 per cent chance of moving to the second stage. Kahneman and Tversky's interpretation is that people do not include this 25 per cent chance of reaching Stage 2 in their calculations of the expected values for Game 1. People are isolating the different options presented to them by focusing their attention, selectively, only on Stage 2 of Game 1.

Building prospect theory

Kahneman and Tversky argued that any decision-making theory should be able to explain the three effects outlined earlier: the *certainty effect*, the *reflection effect*, and the *isolation effect*. Their critique of expected utility theory revolved around the fact that expected utility cannot explain these effects and they decided to develop a theory that could—*prospect theory*. They argued that prospect theory has much more real-world explanatory power than expected utility theory.

Prospect theory is based around the idea that we make judgements about the value of different options in particular ways, which are not consistent with the standard economics approach as captured by expected utility theory. The first insight is about the relative comparisons we make when we are choosing and deciding. We do not decide to buy a new mobile phone based just on all the information we are given about that particular mobile phone and the other new offers—we compare the mobile phone options we are offered with the deal we already have and decide whether or not the new deal is an improvement. We do not start completely afresh when we are making our choices—we compare the options against a starting point—a *reference point*. One implication is that our decisions are driven by *changes* relative to our reference points, and not by all the information we have available to us.

The idea of a reference point develops Kahneman and Tversky's earlier insights about anchoring and adjustment heuristics, discussed in Chapter 4: we anchor our choices around our reference point, and adjust our choices accordingly. As we saw in Chapter 4, often the status quo is our reference point. Kahneman and Tversky link this to the physiological concept of homeostasis which is about how, physiologically, we have a set point and our bodily responses are determined by that set point. The same event will have different impacts on our physiology depending on our starting point: for example, if we are too hot and we feel a blast of cold air, we will find that pleasurable. But if we are too cold and we feel the same blast of cold air, it will be unpleasant. Our choices around our reference points are sticky and less likely to change. We exhibit a lot of inertia in our everyday behaviour. This might be because the effort involved in changing is too much, we procrastinate, we are lazy—there is probably a complex set of socio-economic and psychological reasons to explain our resistance to change.

A second key feature of prospect theory develops from Kahneman and Tversky's insights about the reflection effect covered earlier in this chapter, which links into the concept of loss aversion—we care much more about losses than we do about gains. According to many behavioural economists, one manifestation of loss aversion and the status quo bias is the *endowment effect*. We care much more about the things we have and therefore could lose, than we care about things we do not have and could buy. Daniel Kahneman, Jack Knetsch, and Richard Thaler illustrated the endowment effect in some experiments with students. Students were randomly sorted into different groups including 'buyers' and 'sellers'. The sellers were given mugs—which they could sell. The buyers were given the opportunity to buy mugs. The sellers were asked if they were prepared to sell their mugs at various prices. The buyers were asked if they were prepared to buy at various prices. There was a large difference in sellers' versus buyers' prices: the median price that the sellers were willing to accept was $7.12; the median price that the buyers were willing to pay was $3.12.

Just on the basis of this evidence, we would find it difficult to argue this is definitely the endowment effect at work. You might expect a profit maximizing seller to start with a disproportionately high price, in case they could get away with it. The process of bargaining would see the sellers lowering their willingness to accept and the buyers raising their willingness to pay until an equilibrium is found. Nonetheless, there is evidence that divergences between willingness to pay and willingness to accept are relevant in other choices too.

Demonstrating similar divergences in a wider context, Kip Viscusi and colleagues conducted some experiments on people's attitudes towards chemical poisoning. They showed consumers cans of insecticide and toilet bowl cleaner, and asked people how much they would be willing to pay for a safer product with a lower risk from poisoning. Then people were asked if they would be willing to accept a price reduction on a product with an increased risk of poisoning. Most economists might predict that consumers' responses to these questions should be symmetrical: the amount they are willing to pay for a safer product should be similar in magnitude to the amount of compensation they would expect to get in terms of a price reduction on a relatively unsafe product, but Viscusi and colleagues' experimental findings did not support this conclusion. People's responses to reducing risk exhibited a standard pattern predicted by economic theory: there was a diminishing willingness to pay for higher levels of risk reduction. But people were very unwilling to accept *any* sort of increase in poisoning risk in return for compensation.

Kahneman and Tversky bring their insights together by depicting a *prospect theory value function* to capture our subjective perceptions of value, as illustrated in Figure 3.

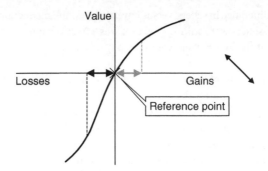

3. The prospect theory value function.

Many of the phenomena identified in this chapter can be seen in the prospect theory value function. It is anchored around a reference point (not necessarily zero). The value function has a sigmoid shape and is not symmetrical around the reference point, reflecting the fact that losses have more impact on value than gains. From looking more closely at Figure 3, we can see the disproportionate impact that losses have in our evaluations of value. The double-headed black arrow illustrates a loss. The double-headed grey arrow illustrates a gain equal in magnitude to the loss. The dashed vertical lines are drawn down to the value function to illustrate the impact of the loss versus the gain on value. The black dashed line is much longer than the grey dashed line: a loss of a given magnitude erodes our perceptions of value much more than an equivalent gain increases our perceptions of value. In this way, loss aversion is captured in the value function, to show how people care much more about losses than equivalent gains. When we lose £100 it upsets us much more than it pleases us to win £100.

Regret theory

Even though it has been very influential in behavioural economics, prospect theory (and its variants) is just one theory that behavioural economists have used. There are others, including

Richard Thaler's mental accounting model and regret theory. Mental accounting builds on some of the ideas about framing and context that emerge from prospect theory, but it also relates to planning about the future—we will explore this model in more detail in Chapter 6.

Graham Loomes and Robert Sugden developed regret theory as an alternative to prospect theory. They argue that regret theory gives us a simpler and more intuitive way than prospect theory to resolve some of the behavioural paradoxes and inconsistencies associated with expected utility theory.

What is the essence of regret theory? Regret theory allows for different states of the world—which we cannot know because we cannot predict what will happen tomorrow. The interaction between our choices today and an unknown future come together to determine how much pleasure (or not) our choices give us, in the end. We regret some decisions; we 'rejoice' in others—but whether or not we regret or rejoice is determined by future states of the world, which might be completely beyond our control. This is a key distinguishing feature of regret theory relative to prospect theory. Prospect theory assumes just one possible state of the world whereas regret theory allows two (or more) states, and our evaluations of our own happiness will depend on which state of the world emerges in the end, and also on our anticipations of future regret.

Imagine that you are deciding whether or not to take an umbrella to work, for example. You have no information about what the weather might be like today (say you live in England). Taking an umbrella involves some hassle—it might not fit easily in your bag; if you are a little absent-minded, umbrellas might be one of the objects you frequently lose. If it rains, however, it will be worth the trouble. So your happiness/satisfaction is determined by something completely beyond your control: the English weather. If it rains you will rejoice at your perspicacity in bringing an umbrella with you. If it is sunny you will regret taking the trouble to pack it, especially if you lose it. Happiness is not dependent just on our perceptions, preferences, and choices. Happiness also depends on how we judge our past choices retrospectively, given the state of the world which unfolds *after* we have made our choices—when it is too late to change our mind. We have no control over these states of the world and yet our happiness is very much dependent upon them.

Economists have studied more serious examples, including the siting of nuclear power plants. If a nuclear power plant is sited in an area where, unexpectedly, there is an earthquake and tsunami (as in Japan in 2011), the planners regret their choice. If there is no earthquake they rejoice at their clever choice of location for the plant. Consequences are determined not only by our own choices but also by events in the world around us.

In this chapter and Chapter 4, we have focused on heuristics, biases, behavioural paradoxes, and the behavioural theories designed to explain them. The focus so far has been mainly on the biases that relate to our decisions and choices in risky situations. Behavioural economists have developed a whole additional literature on the types of biases that emerge when we are deciding over time. Time and risk do interact of course, but for the purpose of this book we will keep it simple and in Chapter 6 we will focus just on the biases that emerge over time.

Chapter 6
Taking time

In Chapters 4 and 5, we focused on risky choices. Another important dimension of our decisions is our attitude towards time. Are we patient? Are we impatient? Or does it depend on the situation? Many of our everyday decisions unfold over time, and what we want today is not always consistent with what we might want tomorrow. How do real people deal with time, and with current decisions that have important future consequences? We are not always good at saving for our pensions in the future. We may struggle to cope with energy bills because we are too fond of turning up the heating or air conditioning, when feeling a little too cold or too hot, without thinking very hard about the consequences in terms of future energy bills. In staying healthy too, we are not always good at planning for the future: with unhealthy habits and lifestyles today we are often storing up health problems for the future.

Standard economic theory does allow that people are different in terms of their *time preference*—or their levels of patience versus impatience. For most economists, people's time preferences can differ *between* individuals but they should be stable *within* individuals. In standard economics, if someone is impatient to get something today and cannot wait until tomorrow, then they will exhibit the same impatience if they are choosing over the same time interval (one day) but rolled forward into the future. This is *time consistency*—our levels of patience versus impatience do not change over time; they are stable. For example, if I am given a choice between chocolate cake today or chocolate cake tomorrow and I choose chocolate cake today then, if I am time consistent, my preference should not change if this same set of choices is rolled forward a year. I should also prefer chocolate cake in a year over chocolate cake in a year and a day. My choices do not change when I am deciding for the near future versus the distant future.

Nor does the standard approach preclude *different* people from making different choices—for example, one person deciding to have their cake sooner rather than later; another later rather than sooner. Again, this is not necessarily inconsistent. Decisions to consume and spend in the very short-term may be strictly rational and consistent, especially if you are facing immediate financial problems and/or your life expectancy is low. For most economists, if people are consistent in favouring smaller rewards sooner over larger rewards later, then they are still strictly rational.

In a study of military personnel and their pension choices, economists Warren and Pleeter found significant individual differences. Military personnel were given two choices: they could take either a large, one-off, lump-sum payment or a small annual payment (an 'annuity') but continuing for the rest of their lives. Warren and Pleeter found that around 51 per cent of the officers chose the lump-sum payment but a much higher proportion of the enlisted personnel—92 per cent—took the lump-sum payment. Warren and Pleeter analysed the data and found that there were significant variations across different groups: white, female, and college-educated groups were more likely to take the annuity. This evidence shows that there are differences across people—which is not a sign of time inconsistency in itself because standard economic theory does not preclude different people having different levels of patience versus impatience. So what can behavioural economics add?

What is time inconsistency?

Behavioural economics draws on evidence from psychology suggesting that the consistency in time preferences, as assumed in standard economic approaches, does not apply for humans (and other animals). We are *disproportionately* impatient in the short-term (we want our chocolate cake today) but when planning for the future, we are more patient (we are prepared to wait a year and a day for our chocolate cake). This is *time inconsistency*—our preferences for delayed outcomes are shifting over time. Our time preferences are not stable. We suffer from *present bias*—we have a disproportionate preference for smaller, immediate rewards over delayed but larger rewards—a reflection of underlying time inconsistency. Our capacity for patience is shifting over time. We are patient in some contexts, but impatient in others. For example—if we have £10 and we are deciding about spending it today, or saving it until next week, we are more likely to spend it today. When we are thinking about more distant decisions, we might be more patient—if we are thinking about spending £10 in a year, or saving it to spend in a year plus one week, then our choices may shift, and we will plan to save for that extra week. Trouble emerges when our impatience today means we have nothing left to spend or save in a year's time, in a decade's time, or when we retire.

Animal models

Some of the early evidence about time inconsistency comes from *animal models*—which draw parallels between our behaviour and other animals' behaviour. Psychiatrist and psychologist George Ainslie observed time inconsistency in a study of pigeons' impulse control. Pigeons were held in a chamber. They could get some food by pecking at keys illuminated with either red or green lights. If they pecked the key when the red light was on, the food rewards were smaller but came sooner. If the green light was on, the rewards were larger but the pigeons had to wait. The pigeons quickly learnt the difference between the rewards they got from pressing green versus red keys, but they were also impulsive—they preferred to peck when the key was red, to get their food more quickly. Other animal behaviourists have identified more constructive, long-term planning behaviour among animals, however. Biologists Mulcahy and Call observed bonobos and orangutans selecting and saving tools to use later, suggesting that they were planning their future actions. Scrub jays and other animals will save and store food too.

Why are we more patient when planning for a distant future? Scott Rick and George Loewenstein explain this in terms of the relative tangibility of benefits versus costs. Today's temptations are hard to resist. Resisting temptation involves tangible short-term costs, and these stop us from achieving future goals. There are numerous examples—dieting, going to the gym, and giving up smoking. We have to forgo an immediate, tangible pleasure—say, of eating chocolate or smoking a cigarette. Or we have to incur some immediate discomfort (e.g. going to the gym and working out). Future goals can seem distant and less tangible, making it harder to exert self-control today. When people fail to control immediate temptations, it can lead to serious problems such as obesity, and drug and gambling addictions, all of which have serious impacts on individuals, families, and public health systems.

The famous *marshmallow experiments*, conducted by psychologist Walter Mischel and his team, illustrate this phenomenon in children's choices. Walter Mischel and his team offered children a range of sweet treats (including marshmallows). If the children were able to resist the temptation to take one treat immediately, they would be rewarded with a second treat later on. The children were able to wait longer if they were distracted, and they also employed their own ways of distracting themselves from temptation. There was also a link with the children's future life chances. The children who were better able to resist temptation demonstrated superior emotional and cognitive function as teenagers, and were more socially and academically competent as adults. The marshmallow experiments inspired Hollywood scriptwriters to create a fictionalized example. In the movie *The Five Year Engagement*, Violet, a psychologist (played by Emily Blunt), decides that her sous chef fiancé Tom (played by Jason Segal) is feckless because he is unable to resist the temptation to eat stale donuts rather than to wait for fresh ones. (Towards the end of the movie, when Tom discovers that Violet had judged him in this way, he defends his behaviour by arguing that there might be all sorts of other reasons to eat stale donuts.)

Intertemporal tussles

Evidence from the marshmallow experiments and other similar studies suggests that our temptations generate internal conflicts. It is as if we are in a struggle with ourselves—as if we have two personalities: a patient self and an impatient self, and these selves are in conflict. Economist Robert Strotz drew on Ainslie's evidence to develop early economic insights about time inconsistency, connecting with this idea of intrapersonal conflict. He postulated that we faced an *intertemporal tussle* between our patient and our impatient selves. While Strotz set out his ideas in great technical detail, it is also an idea that has a lot of intuitive power. Most of us procrastinate about something; many of us probably procrastinate about going to the gym. Our patient self worries about the future—and the impact of a lack of exercise on our future healthiness. Our impatient self likes a comfortable life now, and prefers to sit on the sofa eating chocolate and chips. The net impact will depend on which self dominates.

Neuroeconomic analyses of immediate versus delayed rewards

Neuroscientific tools can be used to capture some of our neural responses when we are facing choices between delayed versus immediate rewards. Sam McClure and colleagues used functional magnetic resonance imaging (fMRI)—a technique for monitoring oxygenated blood flow through the brain and underlying neural areas. They were inspired by Aesop's fable of the ant and the grasshopper to develop a multiple-selves model. The patient ant works hard in the summer, collecting food. The impatient grasshopper enjoys himself by singing away the summer. No prizes for guessing who wins out in the end—when winter comes, the grasshopper begs the ant for food because he is dying of hunger, and the ant tells him to get lost and sing away the winter as he had sung away the summer.

Do we have something like an intertemporal tussle between our ant and our grasshopper selves when we are deciding about immediate versus delayed rewards? To find out, McClure and colleagues asked their experimental participants to value immediate rewards and delayed rewards during a brain scan. They identified different neural activations depending on the timing of rewards. Neural areas associated with high-level cognitive functioning were activated more strongly for delayed rewards. Neural areas associated with more primitive, impulsive instincts were activated more strongly for immediate rewards. They concluded that different neural processes are interacting when we confront choices between immediate, smaller rewards versus delayed, larger rewards, and this could reflect intrapersonal conflicts between multiple selves—a patient planner and an impatient short-termist.

The neuroeconomic evidence is mixed, however. Paul Glimcher and colleagues tested some of the McClure team's assertions. Glimcher's team adjusted the experiment so *all* choices were delayed. The earliest rewards were available only after a sixty-day delay. They found the same patterns as for the McClure study of immediate rewards. Glimcher's team concluded that their evidence demonstrated that time inconsistency is not a reflection of impulsiveness and intertemporal tussles between multiple selves. It is ordinary temptation, and this can be explained in terms of a single self with coherent beliefs and goals.

Pre-commitment strategies and self-control

What is the solution to these self-control problems? Partly it depends on our self-awareness. Ted O'Donoghue and Matthew Rabin argue that some people have more insight into their behaviour than others and they distinguish two broad types: naïve and sophisticated decision-makers—*naïfs* and *sophisticates*. These different types of people will respond to time inconsistency in different ways. Both types will suffer present bias, but the *sophisticates* will be aware that their capacity for self-control is limited, and will implement strategies to force themselves along a more constructive path.

O'Donoghue and Rabin illustrate with an example of students choosing movie trips—the students like to go to the movies on Saturday nights but they have to work on one weekend in the next four weeks because they have an important essay to finish within the month. They have to decide which Saturday they will work instead of going to the movies. O'Donoghue and Rabin set the problem up so that not all the movies in the next four weeks will be the same—the movie in the first week is mediocre, in the next week is good, for the third week it is excellent, and the movie in four weeks will be the best—an outstanding Johnny Depp movie. The optimal choice would be to get the essay done in the first week and go to all the better movies in the subsequent weeks, including the outstanding movie in the fourth week.

The trouble is that students might not have the self-control necessary to ensure this, but the *sophisticates* may do a better job of balancing the trade-offs. The *naïfs* will under-estimate their future self-control problems completely and will procrastinate until the last Saturday and, because they will have an essay to write, they will miss the best, Johnny Depp movie. The *sophisticates* will suffer self-control problems too and will procrastinate a little (they might go to see the mediocre movie in the first week) but they will also have the insight to realize that they might procrastinate too much and miss the best movie. So they prepare themselves by getting the essay done in the second week because they realize that, if they leave it until later, they risk missing out on the Johnny Depp movie. This links to what behavioural economists call a *pre-commitment strategy*: *sophisticates* limit their menu of future choices in order to achieve their long-term goals.

The idea of binding ourselves to ensure we stay on a constructive path is an age-old phenomenon captured in classical literature. In Homer's *Odyssey*, Odysseus (also known as Ulysses) is sailing past the Sirens—mythical creatures who lure sailors to their destruction with their songs. Odysseus ties himself to the mast of his ship while his crew—deafened by wax plugged in their ears—is able to sail by, leaving Odysseus to listen to the Sirens' sweet songs without being seduced into sinking his ship. J. W. Waterhouse illustrated this classical story in his famous painting *Ulysses and the Sirens*—shown in Figure 4. Ulysses' forward-looking self is binding his impatient short-termist self in his attempt to survive.

Coleridge is another example—he realized well the destructive consequences of his opium addiction, so he hired servants to keep him out of opium dens—a far-sighted attempt to bind his immediate desires to indulge his drug habit.

Natural experiments illustrate self-commitment behaviours too. As explained in Chapter 1, natural experiments study real choices and behaviours, not artificial, hypothetical choices as many experimenters are forced to do. DellaVigna and Malmendier studied a set of real data on gym membership. Attendance records showed that people were paying thousands of dollars on annual memberships and then going to the gym only a couple of times—even though they could save a lot of money by using the

4. Ulysses pre-committing himself to resist the Sirens' calls.

cheaper pay-as-you-go option offered by the gym. On the surface, we might think that only a stupid person would pay a lot of money for a gym membership they rarely use—but many of us do exhibit this type of behaviour, and maybe it is not so stupid. Some behavioural economists interpret it as a type of pre-commitment strategy: by spending a lot on a gym membership, we are trying to force our impatient self to be more responsible in the short-term. Our patient self reasons that, if we have spent a lot of money, even our short-termist self will not want to waste it.

Modern businesses now offer services designed around the insight that people's self-control is not perfect. Resisting the temptation of short-term rewards is hard and many of us are prepared to buy our way out of temptation. There are many examples in the dieting world, and also in quitting aids for smokers—most recently e-cigarettes. For anyone who ever has trouble getting up in the morning, they can buy themselves a roaming alarm clock. The original product—Clocky—is an alarm clock that runs around the room so you have to chase it to turn it off, and hopefully by then you will have woken up properly.

The growth of online services has also delivered some pre-commitment services, including Bee-minder and Stikk. The latter offers a service to help people manage their limited self-control problems using financial incentives. Stikk users define their goal online. This forms the basis of a *commitment contract*: if users do not achieve their commitments, then they are charged and the money goes to their chosen beneficiary. Users can make their least favourite charity the beneficiary. If they fail to achieve their goal, a Democrat voter might commit to giving money to the Republicans. Stikk does rely on honest participants, but dishonesty in itself is often a short-termist strategy and how can Stikk devise a watertight contract given that they would find it impossibly difficult and costly to check on their own users' honesty?

BeeMinder is a similar service but with a different underlying business model. BeeMinder offers 'in-your-face' goal tracking for 'flexible self-control'. Like Stikk, their customers set themselves goals to form the basis of their commitment contract with BeeMinder. If they fail to achieve their goal, then BeeMinder charges them. These services can have a powerful impact, especially if they leverage modern technology as a way around the dishonesty problem seen with Stikk. A truly committed BeeMinder client can connect their exercise goals to output from personal fitness monitoring gadgets such as FitBits and iWatches. Technology provides the monitor.

Behavioural life cycle models

If we are not good at saving our money, if our pension pots are not sufficient for us to look after ourselves after retirement, then this will have implications for government budgets and debt. These patterns are explored in behavioural life cycle models, developing David Laibson's insights about how we are disproportionately better at looking after our *golden eggs*—our illiquid stores of wealth which most people hold mainly in the form of pensions and housing wealth—than we are at managing our credit card bills.

Behavioural life cycle models blend behavioural insights about time inconsistency with standard life cycle models assuming time consistency, to study how our patterns of saving, investment, and spending evolve over our lifetimes. George-Marios Angeletos and colleagues used these models in explaining why people might simultaneously hold a lot of credit card debt alongside large stores of illiquid wealth in the form of housing or pensions.

Transaction costs are part of the explanation. Selling a house to settle credit card bills is a complex and expensive process. People have credit cards as a buffer against unexpected bills but, for Angeletos and his colleagues, that is not enough to explain it. They simulate patterns of spending and saving by making some assumptions to match the average experiences of people today, for example that a person will live for a maximum of ninety years, and will work for an average of forty-three years, with household sizes varying over a lifetime as people leave home, marry and have families, and then retire. Then Angeletos and his colleagues use actual data on key variables such as interest rates and employment rates to match their simulations against real-world data about spending and saving patterns. Their findings are consistent with behavioural theories of time inconsistency: the simulated patterns assuming time inconsistency matched real-world macroeconomic trends better than simulated patterns from models incorporating standard economic assumptions about time consistency.

Choice bracketing, framing, and mental accounting

In deciding about consuming today versus tomorrow, the context of our decisions plays a crucial role. For example, as explained in Chapter 5, if a decision is framed as a loss then the final choice may be different from the choice taken when a decision is framed as a gain. How our choices are bracketed together influences our final decision. This forms the basis of another explanation for choices that might seem inconsistent: *choice bracketing*. When we face many complex but related decisions, we may simplify our task by bracketing our choices together.

Richard Thaler developed some of these insights in his model of *mental accounting*. Mental accounting helps to explain why we might not always save as much as we could or should. Framing, reference points, and loss aversion will all determine our perception of our potential spending and saving decisions. Thaler defines mental accounting as the set of cognitive operations we use to organize, assess, and track our financial decisions. Thaler argues that we do not treat all money as equivalent. Money is not *fungible*—we do not perceive it to be exactly the same thing no matter when and where we spend it. How we think about our money and how we spend it will depend on the context in which we win or earn it. We have a set of separate mental accounts and, in our minds, we assign different choices to different accounts. There is a windfall account for money we acquire through lucky events (lottery winnings and other chance events); an income account for the money we earn; and an illiquid wealth account for the money we save.

Our decisions about our money will depend on which mental account we perceive is most relevant. If we win money in a lottery, we might splurge on a treat. If we earned the same money through hard work, then we might be more likely to save it. If we spend large amounts of money online shopping using our credit card, we will perceive that to be cheaper in some sense than paying cash. We treat purchases on credit very differently to cash purchases—possibly partly reflecting poor forward planning too.

Mental accounting means that our evaluation of our economic decisions will depend on the context. We will bracket our choices together and combine choices in our minds. How we perceive a bargain is not determined purely by what we are buying—sometimes the process of shopping, or of finding a bargain, has a value in itself. Thaler illustrates with the example of a woman buying a quilt: all quilts cost the same regardless of size, yet she will buy the biggest quilt even if it is too large for her bed.

Colin Camerer and colleagues explore another manifestation of bracketing: income bracketing and targeting by New York City cab drivers. Camerer and his team were able to get hold of a cab company's daily records of cab drivers' trip sheets and so were able to study working patterns and earnings. Standard economic theory predicts that the cab drivers should maximize their daily earnings, bringing in more on busy days and less on quiet days. They discovered something surprising, however: the cab drivers did not earn more on the busy days. Rather than maximizing their earnings, they were working towards a target and so on busy days they allowed themselves to finish early. Camerer and colleagues offered another explanation too—perhaps cab-drivers were using income targeting as a form of pre-commitment. If a cab driver pre-commits herself to a steady income over time then she will not work extra on busy days because her impatient self might be tempted to splurge her extra income on frivolous spending and trips down the pub. If instead she is working towards a steady target each day, working longer hours on quiet days and shorter hours on busy days, then once in a while, instead of being tempted into excessive spending, she can go home for an early night.

Behavioural development economics

Insights about time inconsistency have been applied in the developing world too. Esther Duflo and her team have used a range of randomized controlled trials (RCTs) to improve agricultural output for poor rural farmers. As explained in Chapter 1, RCTs are a technique borrowed from the medical sciences, where they are used in clinical trials to test the efficacy of drug and other medical interventions. RCTs involve separating participants into two or more groups: a treatment group and a control group. The participants in the control group receive no intervention. The treatment group receives a policy intervention and, to test whether or not the intervention has had an impact, the outcomes for the treatment group are compared to the outcomes for the control group.

In one of their experimental trials, Duflo and her team focused on Kenyan farmers purchasing fertilizer. Fertilizer is relatively expensive in poor rural communities, but if farmers are able to save then they can usually afford the small fixed costs of purchasing fertilizer. The problem in many poor rural regions of the developing world is that the financial infrastructure needed to enable savings (i.e. banks and building societies) does not exist. Without the capacity for saving, farmers may not have the money needed to buy fertilizer because they have to wait for harvest time for their money (a standard economic problem) and cannot use savings from previous harvest income. Another problem might be farmers' present bias: they may procrastinate and postpone their fertilizer purchases. Either way, their agricultural yields will be much lower than they would have been had they bought fertilizer earlier. If, however, the farmers are offered small, time-limited discounts on fertilizer to overcome present bias, and just after the harvest when they have the money to pay for them, then they are more likely to buy the fertilizer they need, leading to significant gains in their agricultural productivity and annual earnings.

Research into time inconsistency and present bias by psychologists, neuroscientists, and evolutionary biologists, as well as behavioural economists and economic psychologists, is some of the most important research in behavioural economics. Most of us know that we struggle to resist temptation, and the standard economic model does not really help us very much because of its unrealistic assumption that we are always cleverly able to make decisions that promote our long-term welfare. Understanding why many people do not behave in a way that is consistent with their own long-term best interests, and what to do about it, is a key challenge for behavioural economists and policy-makers, and the time inconsistency research has a lot to add to these debates.

Chapter 7
Personalities, moods, and emotions

Economists often assume that all people are super-clever and able easily to choose well. As explained in earlier chapters, however, psychological biases lead us to make mistakes more often than standard economics predicts. So far though we have not focused strongly on the underlying psychological reasons, and in this chapter we will explain how and why psychological factors such as personality, mood, and emotions affect our economic and financial decision-making.

This chapter shows the important impacts that personality and emotions have on our working lives, educational attainments, and financial decisions. Some of us are thrill-seekers, looking out for risky opportunities whether in extreme sports, gambling, or financial trading. Others may be risk-averse and cautious—always preferring the safe options. A person who has personality traits associated with higher levels of self-control is able to resist the temptation to spend his money sooner, and is also able to make better life decisions about education and employment.

Personality and emotions have complex impacts because economic circumstances may also feedback into people's emotional states. Moods and emotions will play a role. We are often predisposed to feel particular moods and emotions, driven partly by our personality traits. If we have a more depressed personality, we may be more inclined to feel despondent and resentful when we are cheated in an economic transaction. If we are impulsive, we may be quicker to feel anger, making us more vulnerable to conflicts with our colleagues, friends, and families, and this may affect the opportunities available to us.

Measuring personality

Economic researchers have been slow to incorporate personality into their analyses, perhaps partly because personality is not easy to measure. Psychologists use a wide range of personality tests but economists, so far at least, have used a relatively narrow range. The OCEAN tests are some of the most commonly used tests in behavioural economics. OCEAN was devised by Paul Costa and Robert McCrae and based around the Big Five Model—capturing traits across five dimensions: Openness to experience, Conscientiousness, Extraversion, Agreeableness, and Neuroticism.

Behavioural economists often use cognitive functioning tests too. As for personality, there is a wide range of cognitive functioning tests. One old and widely known cognitive functioning test is Eysenck's (not necessarily particularly accurate) Intelligence Quotient (IQ) test. Behavioural economists in a hurry can use Frederick's cognitive reflexivity test (CRT), which includes questions such as this one: 'A bat and a ball cost $1.10 in total. The bat costs $1.00 more than the ball. How much does the ball cost?' (Think slowly! And see 'References and further reading' for the answer.) The CRT is designed to capture cognitive functioning but also correlates well with people's time and risk preferences. Some people, including highly intelligent people, will jump to an answer, because they are impatient and so do not allow themselves time to think through carefully to the correct answer.

Capturing personality traits is not easy because they are usually measured using self-report questionnaires. These are susceptible to many sources of bias. Experimental participants often want to give answers that make them look good, or impress the experimenter. Feedback between a person's personality and their performance can complicate the results. A neurotic person who is more likely to feel anxious may perform less well in cognitive tests, again not because of impaired ability but because the context of the tests unsettles them. IQ tests require effort and researchers cannot easily discover whether poor performance is a function of a lack of ability, a lack of motivation, or a mixture of both. What experimental participants are paid (or not) will also affect their personality measurements. When children are offered treats, their performance in IQ tests improves—the treats do not make children cleverer, but they do motivate them to try harder. Adults are affected by motivation too. Emotionally stable, conscientious participants may be less affected by additional external incentives such as money payments—and so measuring their cognitive functioning may be easier.

Personality and preferences

Once we have measured a person's personality, what are the economic implications? Economists often assume that people's choices are driven by their preferences, and personality plays a role. An empathetic person is probably more likely to make altruistic choices. Impulsive people are more likely to be impatient and may not be so good at saving up for their retirement, for example. Venturesome people are more likely to take risks, which might lead them into particular choices—they will be more likely to gamble and/or take risky jobs.

Genes also play a role. David Cesarini and colleagues studied twins—identical twins (with the same genes) and non-identical twins (with different genes). They compared the two groups to pick up the impacts of variations in genetic versus environmental factors on risk preferences. Only 20 per cent of the variation in generosity and risk-seeking behaviours across the different twins could be attributed to genetic factors. In one study, Cesarini and colleagues found that about 16 to 34 per cent of the variations in the twins' over-confidence was linked to genetic make-up. In another study of pension plans, they found that 25 per cent of the variations in the riskiness of financial portfolios selected by twins could be attributed to genetic factors.

Personality and cognition

Our personalities have an impact on many of our economic and financial decisions and choices. Often making decisions requires some thought, and our personality traits can determine our cognitive skills and, through our cognition, drive our choices. The consequences often unfold over a lifetime because they determine our academic achievements, job performance, and social skills. If a conscientious person is inclined to be more patient, then they may also be more willing to save for their retirement and/or invest in themselves, for example by getting a good education.

In Chapter 6 we looked at Walter Mischel's marshmallow experiments and the evidence correlating a child's ability to exert self-control and resist temptation with her later success. Mischel and colleagues found that children who were able to resist temptation were more successful later in life. Other studies have shown that the children who were less able to resist temptation were more likely to engage in criminality later in life.

Lex Borghans and colleagues also conducted some very thorough research into personality and life chances. They found that conscientiousness was correlated with academic achievement, job performance, leadership, and longevity. But there is not one unique set of personality traits that guarantees us success in our economic and social lives. Different personality traits are valuable in different places. At work, we generally prefer to have trustworthy colleagues. At a party, we are probably more interested in whether or not someone has a sense of humour. Different personalities suit different jobs. When we are ill, we want our doctors to be empathetic and reliable with good cognitive skills so they are able easily to make an accurate link between our symptoms and their diagnosis. On the other hand, when we go to a restaurant, we want our chefs to be inventive and inspired—we might even believe that they will create more delicious food if they are temperamental, imaginative, and volatile. We probably do not want our doctors to be temperamental, imaginative, or volatile.

Personality in childhood

Personality affects our lives from a very early age, and personality and cognition in very young children can be malleable. Environment has an important influence. Lex Borghans and colleagues found that children adopted by parents with high socio-economic status have larger gains in IQ points than children whose adoptive parents are from lower socio-economic groups. Children from disadvantaged backgrounds can also be helped by access to good childcare centres and home visits. These interventions are designed to help children develop good cognitive skills, but they also succeed in effectively boosting social and personality skills. Well-designed educational interventions can help children to develop complex skills requiring effort and practice. Once they have acquired these skills, then their economic success later in life will hopefully be improved too.

Personality and motivation can be as crucial to early success as cognitive ability and IQ. Economics Nobel laureate Jim Heckman and colleagues studied some of these influences using evidence from a US study of educational interventions—the HighScope Perry Preschool Study. This scheme was designed for children from disadvantaged African-American backgrounds. The curriculum focused on developing the children's cognitive and socio-emotional skills via active, open-ended learning and problem solving. Heckman and his team monitored the children's subsequent success and compared their outcomes to those of a control group (who had not had access to the HighScope intervention).

The positive impacts from this intervention declined as the children got older, and the benefits for disadvantaged children were much higher than for other groups. Heckman and his colleagues estimated that the benefits from the interventions were large. The children on the scheme went on to do much better in adulthood. They were less likely to get a criminal record or be dependent on benefits later in life. They achieved more highly in terms of their educational attainment, employability, and earnings. Heckman and his team estimated that the overall rate of return from the investment in the HighScope intervention was around 7–10 per cent. These days, most advanced economy governments can borrow at rates around 1 per cent and lower; if Heckman's figures are indicative, a government willing to borrow some money to spend on similar educational interventions, especially those targeted specifically at disadvantaged groups, will be spending public money wisely.

Emotions, moods, and visceral factors

Economist Jon Elster is one of the pioneers in the study of how moods and emotions affect economic decision-making. What is the difference between moods and emotions? Elster describes emotions as having a target, while moods are more diffuse and less directed. Moods may also be collectively experienced and in this sense moods are less affected by personality traits than emotions. We will say some more about moods in the macroeconomy in Chapter 8 because moods link to confidence and sentiment, both of which are key drivers of macroeconomic fluctuations and financial market instability.

Emotions, especially our social emotions, can be more highly evolved than our basic instincts. Even so, economists often think of emotions as an irrational element in our decision-making. Challenging this assumption, Elster and others explain how emotions and rationality can complement each other. Emotions are important 'tie-breakers' when we are feeling indecisive. Emotions often help us to decide efficiently because they can operate quickly. But in other situations they are not so helpful—for example, we often feel fear when we confront risky, uncertain situations and this can paralyse us when we need to act.

The affect heuristic

Emotions have a complicated impact on our economic and financial choices, but we can understand these complexities better by connecting emotions and heuristics. As explained in Chapter 4, heuristics are quick decision-making rules and often they guide us well, but sometimes they lead us into mistakes. Biases emerge when people use the availability heuristic, focusing on information that is easy to remember whilst ignoring less memorable, but potentially more important, objective information. Emotions play a role in this too. Emotions are more easily accessible and available to us than objective facts and figures. Emotions are often vivid and we can remember them more easily. They are also associated with quicker, more automatic responses. Emotions affect memories and so will determine what is remembered and what is forgotten. So we use emotions to guide our actions—they are integral to a type of heuristic known as the *affect heuristic*.

Emotions and the affect heuristic can also interfere with our cognitive processing. This is something that advertisers and sensationalist journalism exploit. Vivid imagery is easy to remember. When we see vivid, frightening depictions, for example of plane hijacks and crashes, it might lead us to decide to avoid plane flights when it is in fact more risky to take a train. People who have witnessed horrific car crashes may have distorted perceptions of the risk of driving, reflecting their previous emotional responses on witnessing accidents. This may lead them to decide not to drive a car, when the chances of an accident as a pedestrian are greater.

Basic instincts and visceral factors

Elster distinguishes emotions from *visceral factors*. Visceral factors link to our basic instincts, for example hunger and thirst. They are innate and often operate beyond our conscious control. Visceral factors are like emotions in that they help us to decide quickly. They are essential to human survival and basic daily functioning, but they are also powerful and can crowd out our other goals because they are more primitive and hard-wired, and less evolved than our emotions.

Amongst others, psychologist Joseph le Doux and behavioural economist George Loewenstein have done a lot of work explaining how emotions and visceral factors contribute to self-destructive behaviour. Loewenstein argues that we are more shortsighted and selfish when our visceral factors are driving us, and we are less altruistic when visceral factors are intense. They limit our capacity for empathy too: when deciding for others, we ignore/under-weight their visceral factors. We imagine that others experience our visceral factors in the same way that we experience them, yet we also under-estimate the impact of other people's visceral factors on their behaviour. Visceral factors can help to explain why we indulge in risk-taking and self-destructive behaviours, such as addiction. Partly the problem is that our visceral factors are magnified in our modern, artificial environments. Today's technologies allow us to make many of our decisions much, much more quickly than our distant ancestors could because we have computers and the Internet. For most people in advanced economies, food is abundant, and quick to buy and eat, as are many addictive substances. In the modern world, we may no longer want or need to be driven by quick, instinctive impulses. Problems are compounded when we lack insight into the role that visceral factors play in our decisions when we under-weight or ignore them.

All this means that visceral factors can have confusing and complicated impacts on our decisions and choices. They may conflict with our higher level cognitive functioning, and they may disrupt our interactions and relationships with other people. Neuroscientist Jonathan Cohen has a relatively optimistic view of this. He argues that, in evolutionary terms, we have been quite adaptable. Reason and control developed at the same time as our social and physical environments changed rapidly, and our old emotional processes became maladapted as technology developed. Impulsive, emotional responses may have played an important survival role when we were hunter-gatherers—basic resources were scarce and perishable, so quick, instinctive action was essential to avoid starvation. In a modern context these instincts may not serve a useful purpose and may in fact generate perverse behaviour such as addictions. Cohen argues that, in spite of all this maladaptation, evolution has 'vulcanized' and strengthened the brain so that reason and control can balance primitive emotional responses. As such, it has allowed humans to develop some of the pre-commitment devices mentioned in Chapter 6—for example, savings plans, smokers' nicotine gum, and e-cigarettes. In this way, our brains have evolved to moderate the influence of impulsive, self-destructive, emotional decision-making.

The somatic marker hypothesis

Neuroscientist Antonio Damasio also takes a more positive view of the role emotions play in driving our choices. Emotions are associated with important physiological cues manifested in our bodily responses—what Damasio calls *somatic markers*. Knowledge from somatic markers is communicated via our emotions, and sometimes this helps us to make better decisions faster—as noted earlier, emotions drive the affect heuristic.

Somatic markers may be the outcome of conscious thought. More often, though, they operate unconsciously. For example, if we have been burnt in a fire, when we see fires we become fearful and so we stay away. This is an example of how somatic markers translate into emotions that trigger actions. Other somatic markers are more conscious—for example, the gut feel of entrepreneurs who just 'know' intuitively that an investment will work well—in some senses gut feel represents conscious feelings about choices and plans. When experts have a hunch—for example, when a doctor suspects that their patient is suffering from a specific disease without being able to set out their reasoning clearly—they just have a feeling or intuition that represents the sum of all their knowledge and experience.

Damasio and his colleagues focus their research on patients with brain damage, including one of history's best-known lesion patients—Phineas Gage, who worked on the railroads in the USA. One day an iron rod shot into his brain. In one way, Phineas Gage was very lucky—he recovered with no obvious external physical damage. However, the accident had damaged his frontal lobe (usually associated with higher level cognitive functioning). As well as making significant changes to his personality, this brain damage impaired Phineas Gage's working ability. He eventually lost his job and suffered various other economic and emotional hardships. Antonio Damasio saw similar patterns in his own patients, including Elliot, who had suffered frontal lobe damage after an operation to remove a brain tumour. Like Phineas Gage, Elliot's basic cognitive functioning was good in many ways, but he became extremely obsessive. His emotional responses were impaired and, apart from the social consequences, this affected his economic life too because he found it very difficult to make choices when faced with a range of options. Damasio suggests that this is because emotions help us to decide between different options: Elliot's damaged emotional responses were connected with his inability to choose and decide. The constraints on his emotional responses severely impaired his productivity at work.

Attributing these behaviours to emotional influences is difficult, however, because emotions are not easy to measure and observe.

Dan Ariely and his team devised a novel way to try and capture emotional influences by giving experimental participants visual information—in colour and in black and white. Their idea was that coloured pictures are more vivid and therefore can trigger a stronger emotional response. They also manipulated their participants' perceptions via a series of 'priming' exercises: they asked the participants to recall different events in their past in which their emotions had helped them to make good decisions. The participants were also asked to recall events in their past in which their cognitive capacity had helped them to choose well. Then the participants were given a series of choices for different products. They found that when participants did not have great faith in their own cognitive capacity, they relied more on emotions; when they trusted their feelings, they also relied more on emotions; and when they had colour photos, they relied more on emotions. Ariely's team found that the participants were more likely to choose consistently when they were deciding about products eliciting a stronger emotional response. This evidence confirms some of Antonio Damasio and others' insights about emotions: they can have a positive impact and can help us to make good decisions. Emotions are not irrational.

Dual-system models

How can we reconcile all these differing views about whether or not emotions are useful? Some of the complexities and apparent contradictions are reconciled in *dual-system models*—which capture the interactions between emotion/affect versus cognition. In *Thinking, Fast and Slow*, Daniel Kahneman summarizes the work he has done in this area, and its connection with his earlier work with Amos Tversky on heuristics, bias, and prospect theory—as explored in Chapters 4 and 5. He envisages our thinking processes as a type of map, separating two main different decision-making systems—the automatic, quick, and intuitive System 1; and the cognitive, deliberative, controlled System 2.

The research on systems thinking in behavioural economics is large and growing, with many experiments designed to capture some of the influences. Following from the studies of incentives and motivations explored in Chapter 2, Dan Ariely and colleagues explored the idea that money incentives can impair our performance, because they shift our attention from effective automatic processes. For example, professional sports people tend to play better when they are not thinking too hard about how they are moving. Big prizes in high profile international sporting competitions such as Wimbledon can lead to *choking under pressure*. Ariely and his team did some experiments in the USA and India. Their experimental participants worked on different tasks and were paid according to how they performed, but those who were paid most generously did not necessarily perform the best. They postulated that participants choked under pressure when playing for large rewards because these rewards triggered perverse emotional responses and conflicts between affect and cognition, which impaired the participants' performance.

Some behavioural economists develop these ideas as an alternative to the visceral factor models of addiction, described by Loewenstein and le Doux. Both groups of theories are alternatives to the *rational addiction* models of mainstream economists including those from Gary Becker and colleagues, who argued that most of what we do, including addiction, is the outcome of a rational choice. This is hard to reconcile with our personal experiences of addiction. Dual systems models are more intuitively powerful in capturing what drives addiction. One key set of insights is seen in Bernheim and Rangel's model of *hot-cold states*. Our emotions and visceral factors are more likely to overwhelm us when we are in a 'hot' state, feeling stressed, than when we are in a 'cold' state, feeling calm. In a hot state, we are more likely to misjudge situations, and to be susceptible to temptation. For recovering addicts, this can trigger relapses into addiction. David Laibson illustrates with an example of a cocaine addict who was able to recover from his addiction whilst in prison but relapsed as soon as he was released—he was returning to places and cues that he associated with his old addictive habits.

Our emotions have wider impacts too—affecting our political as well as our economic lives. Writing in the UK newspaper *The Telegraph* in advance of the UK's 2016 referendum vote on whether or not Britain should 'Brexit' (i.e. leave the European Union), Daniel Kahneman's insights about how irritation and anger could increase the chances of a Brexit vote were prescient. In the run-up to the vote, emotions dominated the analysis. After a Brexit vote, emotions were heightened again with many 'Remainers' reporting a feeling of depression and loss at an event that did not affect themselves or their families personally, at least not immediately. Perhaps other behavioural influences such as loss aversion were driving emotional responses too.

Emotions in neuroeconomics

Measuring emotions is very complicated, even more so than measuring personality. Neuroscientists have been working on emotions for much longer than economists and some of their tools are useful when studying economic and financial decision-making, and economists and neuroscientists are coming together in an innovative branch of behavioural economics—*neuroeconomics*. Neuroeconomists combine theories and tools from economics and neuroscience. Neuroscience has a lot to offer economists, particularly in the form of new and innovative sources of data. Some experimenters link economic and financial decision-making to measurements of physiological responses—including heart rate, skin conductance and sweat rates, as well as eye tracking. For example Smith and Dickhaut used heart rate data to infer emotional states in auction experiments.

Measuring general physiological responses cannot give us very detailed information about emotional responses. Brain imaging gives richer information, but it also involves expensive and

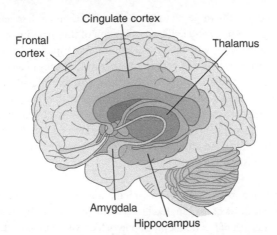

Cingulate cortex

Frontal cortex

Thalamus

Amygdala

Hippocampus

5. Some brain regions. The amygdala is part of the limbic system, a network of interconnected brain structures traditionally associated with the processing of emotion.

complicated techniques. Samples from brain-imaging experiments are usually very small, especially in comparison with the very large sample sizes used in other areas of economics. One of the most commonly used brain-imaging techniques is functional magnetic resonance imaging (fMRI). This has been used in a few neuro-finance experiments, especially to capture links between risky decision-making and emotions. Other experiments have used brain-imaging techniques to study participants' emotional and cognitive responses in social situations, a way to test the dual-systems models described earlier. These experiments are based around a loose categorization of different neural areas and their role in emotional versus cognitive processing.

A classic example is the experiments conducted by Sanfey and colleagues. They used neuroscientific techniques to capture interactions of emotion and cognition when people play the Ultimatum Game, explained in Chapter 3. To recap on the structure of the Ultimatum Game: a proposer makes an offer to responder, if the responder rejects this offer then neither gets anything. In Sanfey and colleagues' version of this experiment, in some rounds of the game the experimental participants played with people they had met earlier. In other rounds they played against a computer. Unsurprisingly perhaps, unfair offers from human proposers were rejected more frequently than unfair offers from computers. Participants reported some relatively extreme emotional responses. They reported feeling angry when they were made an unfair offer, and they were prepared to sacrifice financial gain to punish their co-player.

The participants in Sanfey's experiments were scanned using fMRI to measure flows of oxygenated blood through different brain areas. Briefly, this sort of brain mapping approach draws on the idea that different brain areas are implicated in different types of thinking. The pre-frontal cortex is a more highly evolved area of the brain usually associated with higher cognitive functioning. Paralleling Kahneman's mapping of different thinking systems, the pre-frontal cortex is implicated in System 2 cognitive and controlled thinking. Figure 5 illustrates the frontal cortex and some of the other brain regions associated with emotional processing—in what is sometimes called the *emotional limbic system*.

Sanfey and colleagues focus on a brain region known as the insula—which is often associated with emotional processing of negative emotional states such as pain, hunger, thirst, anger, and disgust. It is a part of the limbic system but is located deep within the brain and so is not easy to illustrate here. The insula is implicated in the impulsive, automatic styles of decision-making associated with System 1 thinking. For Sanfey and colleagues' study of responses in the Ultimatum Game, they found that the insula was more strongly activated with unfair offers from humans than with those from computers, and the more unfair the offer the greater the insula response. The participants' insula activations also had predictive power: participants with stronger insula activations went on to reject a much larger proportion of the unfair offers. Sanfey and colleagues suggested that perhaps the participants were responding in the same way to unfair offers as they would to a bad smell—unfair treatment was generating a 'moral' type of disgust as well as anger.

The participants' pre-frontal cortex was more strongly activated with unfair offers that were subsequently accepted—perhaps because unfair offers are more difficult to accept and it was taking cognitive strength to overcome an emotional impulse to reject them. Another interesting finding from the Sanfey study was that there seemed to be an umpire in this conflict—an area known as the anterior cingulate cortex, commonly associated with conflict resolution. The cingulate cortex is also illustrated in Figure 5. Perhaps it was activated because it was playing a role in resolving the conflict between the cognitive versus emotional responses. Our cognitive system wants the money; the emotional system wants to punish the proposer if they are mean. The anterior cingulate cortex resolves this intraneural conflict.

Other neuroeconomic studies explore our empathetic responses. Again using brain-imaging techniques, Tania Singer and colleagues conducted some experiments showing that, when experimental participants observe their partner receiving painful electrical shocks, their empathetic responses engage automatic emotional processing circuits including the insula. Empathetic responses seem to be generated by making representations of our own internal feeling states in response to pain observed in others.

Neuroeconomic experiments on financial decision-making

Some neuroeconomic studies explore the impact of emotions on financial markets. Researchers have studied the financial decisions of lesion patients—people who have suffered brain damage. Baba Shiv and colleagues studied the behaviour of a panel of lesion patients and compared it with the decisions of ealthy controls. Both groups were asked to play a financial investment game. The healthy participants quickly learnt to select less risky strategies. The lesion patients took much greater risks, but earned significantly more. Other studies have found that people experiencing intense emotional reactions behave differently in financial trading games—Andrew Lo and colleagues found that experimental participants experiencing more extreme emotional responses were less effective as financial traders.

Brain-imaging studies have also shown a relationship between emotional states and traders' behaviour. Brian Knutson and colleagues conducted some brain-scanning studies using fMRI on traders who were choosing between safe and risky stocks. Knutson and colleagues found that emotional processing played an important role in financial decisions: risky choices were associated with activations in a brain area known as the striatum—which is implicated in our processing of rewards, including rewards from risk-taking and addiction. They also found significant differentials in the activation of the insula depending on whether the traders were playing for safe versus risky options. This could reflect the insula's role in negative emotional states, including fear of loss—if fears of loss are associated with risk-avoiding mistakes.

Our hormones may also play a role. Neuroscientist Joe Herbert and economist John Coates were able to conduct a natural experiment looking at the behaviour of a group of London day-traders—traders looking to profit from fluctuations in asset prices over the course of a day.

Coates and Herbert used saliva samples to measure the traders' testosterone and cortisol levels. Testosterone is thought to be associated with greater risk-taking and anti-social behaviour; and cortisol levels are higher when we are feeling more stressed. Coates and Herbert found that the traders' testosterone levels in the morning correlated with their performance later in the day—traders with higher testosterone levels in the morning seemed to earn more profits from their trading over the day. Perhaps this suggests that risk-taking and ruthlessness are driven, at least partly, by our physiology and not by a process of rational calculation as described in standard economic analyses.

Other studies have used insights from psychoanalysis. David Tuckett is a psychoanalyst who has used some of his expertise to study traders' emotions. Tuckett suggests that the financial assets with which traders are preoccupied are not just valuable in money terms. They are what psychoanalysts call *phantastic objects*—objects that their owners believe have superlative, exceptional qualities. Emotional conflict is created when the excitement from making money is separated in time from the panic-inducing fear of losses. Traders make their profits in one phase, and lose their money in another. This might partly explain how a speculative bubble grows: traders forget quickly about past losses. They construct stories and narratives to rationalize their impulsivity. Euphoric booms are followed by emotional oscillations concluding in spectacular collapses of confidence as bubbles burst—triggered initially, according to Tuckett, by traders' emotional conflicts.

This role of emotions in trading behaviour might explain some of the financial instability that impairs macroeconomic performance. In Chapter 8 we explore some of these themes in the context of a relatively new and uncharted territory for behavioural economists—behavioural macroeconomics.

Chapter 8
Behaviour in the macroeconomy

In Chapter 7, we explored the role played by emotions in economic and financial decision-making. When we look at these emotional and psychological factors in aggregate, it has implications for the development of some new macroeconomic models designed to analyse how these socio-psychological influences drive our collective behaviours. The economic behaviour of us all together, as bit players in the macroeconomy, is a crucial issue for policy-makers but it is also the area of economics that is most misunderstood. Since the financial crises of 2007/2008, the credibility of traditional macroeconomic models has been strained. This chapter will explore how behavioural economists can contribute to the development of innovative macroeconomic theories, and to the collection of new types of behavioural macroeconomic data.

Behavioural macroeconomics is a relatively undeveloped field because it suffers from some significant constraints, partly reflecting the difficulty of bringing together the choices of lots of different types of people all with different personalities, experiencing different moods, emotions and deciding in complex ways using a wide range of heuristics generating an even wider range of biases. So behavioural economists tend to focus on the microeconomic behaviour of consumers, workers, business people or policy-makers. Even this is difficult because, as explained in

Chapter 8, it is not easy to measure personality, moods, and emotions. So the analytical task is enormous for behavioural macroeconomists because the problems of behavioural measurement are compounded by the many and complex ways in which individuals interact within a macroeconomy.

When we pull all our choices together, this has implications for headline variables usually the focus of everyday macroeconomic news stories, including employment, unemployment, output and production growth, inflation, and interest rates. Moods and emotions affect the well-being of all of us together, and policy-makers are realizing this more and more. They are designing new macroeconomic policy goals to capture some of these insights. The macroeconomy is no longer solely the territory for economists. Insights from psychology, psychiatry, sociology, medicine, and public health are showing us that the welfare of a nation is not just about the monetary circumstances of its citizens. Later in this chapter we will explore some of these themes.

The psychology of the macroeconomy

Behavioural macroeconomics focuses on how social and psychological factors, including optimism and pessimism, can help us to understand macroeconomic fluctuations. Entrepreneurs are often driven by economy-wide fluctuations in mood and business confidence, and this affects how quickly the businesses grow and whether or not business people are prepared to invest in new business projects—with implications for macroeconomic output and growth. When the business world is feeling optimistic, then this can be a self-fulfilling prophecy, driving rises in national output overall.

Attitudes towards time are important too because macroeconomic fluctuations are driven by people's decisions to consume today or save for the future. Whether consumers are generally patient or impatient determines whether or not they are inclined to spend save today. If they are more patient and save more, then this can generate funds for entrepreneurs' new investment projects. If consumers are more impatient and consume more, this can boost economic activity in the short-term as businesses expand their production to meet consumers' demands. Business entrepreneurs must decide whether or not to invest in growing their businesses in the future. Put all these decisions together and they have significant implications for the macroeconomy as a whole.

Our psychology will interact with our attitudes towards the future too. Emotion and moods determine whether or not we are inclined to make forward-looking decisions. Hope and optimism, along with confidence, propel economies forward partly because the business entrepreneurs who play a key role in building economies' productive capacity are vulnerable to shifts in confidence and sentiment. The 2016 UK referendum vote on whether or not Britain should leave the European Union (to 'Brexit', or not to 'Brexit') was a stark illustration of this—when the voters to leave (the 'Brexiteers') won, many of those who voted to remain in the EU, amongst them a majority of UK business leaders and economists, were struck by a profound sense of pessimism. The immediate macroeconomic consequences were profound. Along with the economic, political, and financial uncertainty following the vote, the pound plummeted and many investors pulled out of the UK. The negative consequences for the UK economy were felt quickly.

Whether we are patient versus impatient and optimistic versus pessimistic will determine whether or not we feel positive about the future, which in turn will also affect how patient or impatient we are. Tali Sharot, an experimental psychologist, has shown that we seem to be naturally inclined towards optimism—we seem to have evolved a tendency to be over-optimistic with most healthy people being prone to an optimism bias. The EU Referendum also illustrated this tendency—many voters for remaining in the EU expressed surprise and shock at the result, even though many polls, for many weeks, had been predicting that the Brexiteers would win the vote, even if narrowly.

Optimism bias affects public investment in construction and infrastructure too, something recognized by the UK's Audit Office, which monitors government spending on projects. In 2013, the Audit Office conducted a study of over-optimism in the construction sector. It found that it was linked to inflated costs for government projects because planners were not always realistic about the future prospects for their projects, and so they under-estimated costs and were insufficiently realistic about potential delays.

Economists John Ifcher and Homa Zarghamee used two empirical tools to capture some of the links between optimism and patience. They analysed self-reported levels of happiness from the US General Social Survey. Respondents who were in a more positive state of mind were also more patient and reported that they were less likely to 'live for today'. Ifcher and Zarghamee also conducted an experiment to capture the impact of emotions on people's attitudes towards the future. One group was shown happy film-clips—for example, they were asked to watch a stand-up comic's routine. A second group was shown neutral films—for example, clips of wildlife and landscapes. Then all participants were asked to state how much they valued making payments today to invest in their future. The group that had watched the comedy routine exhibited more patience—they valued investments in their future more highly than did the other group, which may suggest that a happy mood makes us more interested in the future.

Early behavioural macroeconomists: Katona, Keynes, and Minsky

The focus on emotions as drivers of macroeconomies is not new. George Katona was one of the forefathers of economic psychology and many of his insights resonate with modern versions of behavioural macroeconomics. He observed that emotional factors (e.g. nervousness or euphoria) can induce shifts in consumer sentiment, investor confidence, and aggregate demand in ways not captured by standard macro economic models.

John Maynard Keynes also had a profound influence. In chapter 12 of his 1936 book *The General Theory of Employment, Interest and Money*, Keynes describes two main sets of actors driving the macroeconomy: speculators and entrepreneurs. Each group has a distinctive personality, and is affected differently by emotions. Financial speculators chase financial returns—they want to maximize their profits from buying and selling financial assets.

Keynes focused his analysis on speculators' behaviour in share and stock markets. The rapid growth of financial technologies, especially since the 1980s, has meant that stocks and shares are not the only risky financial assets available today, but Keynes's basic logic holds in modern financial markets too. Stock markets provide liquidity, which is good in the sense that it provides funds for business entrepreneurs to build their productive capacity, but this liquidity means that stocks and shares are very quick and easy to buy and sell. Financial speculators chase short-term profits and so they focus only on the very short-term fluctuations in share prices. They are also driven strongly by what other speculators are doing.

Keynes postulates that speculators will often believe that others might know more about the potential profits from a stock and so will copy others when they are buying and selling, especially if they are not very sure of market trends. Speculators are preoccupied with what others think because this determines the price they should pay for shares. Speculators are not so worried about a share's fundamental value in terms of what it could earn over its lifetime. They are more worried about the price they will get for the share in the very near future. For this, other speculators' opinions are most important because, potentially, they could be buying the shares tomorrow.

Keynes uses the metaphor of a newspaper *beauty contest* to capture this preoccupation with others' opinions. He describes a competition in which contestants are asked to examine a number of pictures of pretty women, however their task is not to select the one they think is prettiest but the one they think *others* will think is prettiest. Essentially they must second-guess the other contestants' judgements—thus creating a situation of contestants judging what others think others are thinking about others' decisions. For the macroeconomy, Keynes argues that when speculators are following these conventions and playing beauty contest games, then their valuations of shares will have no strong basis in real beliefs. This contributes to instability and volatility—with macroeconomic consequences, because an atmosphere of instability and uncertainty deters the entrepreneurs from investing to build their businesses.

Entrepreneurs are the other group of personalities in Keynes's macroeconomy. For Keynes, business and entrepreneurship are not just about making money—if you want to make money, speculation offers relatively large and predictable rewards because speculators focus their activities over the very short-term. Often speculators are most concerned about how share prices will fluctuate over a day, week, or month. Speculators are not generally focused on what happens to share prices over years and decades (though financial investment guru, Warren Buffett, is a notable exception).

Entrepreneurs face a much more tricky task than speculators. They have to think more carefully about the long-term, which is difficult because the future can be so uncertain. A perfectly rational entrepreneur would invest very little in their business if they had to rely on purely mathematical calculations to back up their investment decisions. Uncertainty about the future, especially innovative businesses, means that it is hard to predict how well our business might be doing in a year, five years, or a decade. For entrepreneurs something else overcomes uncertainty and fears about the future: *animal spirits*. Animal spirits can be understood partly in terms of optimism bias discussed earlier, as analysed by Tali Sharot and others. Galen of Pergamon, a Greek physician to the gladiators in ancient Rome, first developed the concept of *animal spirits*. He described animal spirits as connecting our internal neurophysiology with our actions, and his ideas were the basis of Hippocrates' description of the four humours—black bile, yellow bile, blood, and phlegm—each associated with a particular temperament: melancholic, choleric, sanguine, and phlegmatic, respectively.

Keynes's animal spirits link to the sanguine temperament—they are about the desire to act and to do something positive. Making the leap from the ancient to the modern world, Galen's animal spirits may also capture a spontaneous optimism associated with the animal spirits of entrepreneurs, which propels them to feeling confident about the future and to investing in building their businesses. What has this got to do with the macroeconomy? Keynes explains that the balance between the activities of the entrepreneurs versus those of the speculators will determine the impact of the stock market on macroeconomic variables including output, employment, unemployment, and growth. Animal spirits are easily dimmed by uncertainty and instability, however. So when financial markets are volatile, entrepreneurs feel unsettled and they will be much less willing to invest in building their businesses for the future.

The financial system connects the entrepreneurs and the speculators. Entrepreneurs need funds from financial markets to build their businesses in the long-term, and financial markets can provide the funds they need. Keynes argues that all will go well when these tendencies are in balance, when speculation is just a bubble on the steady stream of enterprise. However, if speculation becomes an unstable whirlpool, then it will destabilize the macroeconomy, magnifying volatility and uncertainty.

Modern behavioural macroeconomics: the animal spirit models

As previously noted, aggregating from individuals' decisions to capture macroeconomic phenomena is particularly tricky for behavioural macroeconomists. Behavioural macroeconomists can find it difficult to bring together all the complex influences and personalities that drive individuals into a coherent aggregate macroeconomic model. Conventional macroeconomics escapes these complications by assuming that all workers and all businesses are the same, deciding in the same way. Also, everyone is perfectly rational so it is relatively easy to describe how different people interact in the macroeconomy. Standard macroeconomic theories describe one person—*a representative agent*, who makes their decisions in a relatively simple way. In many standard macroeconomic theories, the representative agent captures the behaviour of all firms or all workers. Multiply the representative agents' behaviour and you get your macroeconomic model. In this analysis the macroeconomy is strongly grounded on microeconomic principles.

Behavioural macroeconomists cannot convincingly aggregate using the device of rational representative agents in the same way because the essence of behavioural economics is to capture differences in personality and emotions, and in interactions between agents. There is no single representative agent in behavioural economics. Instead, behavioural macroeconomists tend to focus on aggregate phenomena—for example, business confidence and consumer confidence.

Another way in which modern behavioural macroeconomists build their models is by focusing on specific psychological motivators of action, often employing the concept of animal spirits, but defined in different ways from Keynes's and Galen's definitions. Akerlof and Shiller, in their book *Animal Spirits*, describe a range of animal spirits that affect the macroeconomy and financial systems. Their definition of animal spirits is much less precise than Keynes's. Essentially they equate animal spirits with a range of psychological phenomena whereas Keynes's concept was more about the gut instincts of entrepreneurs investing in building their productive capacity. For Akerlof and Shiller, animal spirits go beyond the animal spirits of entrepreneurs to include a set of five animal spirits, each with its own destabilizing influence—including confidence, preferences for fairness, corruption, money illusion, and storytelling.

Other modern behavioural macroeconomists have developed sophisticated mathematical models around animal spirits, incorporating a definition that is different again from Keynes's original macroeconomic application of Galen's concept. Macroeconomists including Roger Farmer, Paul de Grauwe, and Michael Woodford model animal spirits cycles using sophisticated mathematical techniques, essentially capturing animal spirits as random fluctuations (*random noise*) driving the macroeconomy to switch from buoyant to recessionary states of the world.

Finance and the macroeconomy

Behavioural macroeconomists also focus on the impact of finance and financial instability. Many mainstream macroeconomic theories neglect the financial sector, but since the 2007/8 financial crises and the subsequent global recessions, economists and policy-makers are being reminded how important the financial sector is to macroeconomic performance. One place to start is the psychology of speculative bubbles. Historical accounts of speculative bubbles are difficult to reconcile with the standard economic view of calmly rational agents making careful mathematical calculations when assessing the relative benefits and costs of buying an asset. Tulipmania, one of the most colourful episodes in financial history, illustrates how unstable and irrational a speculative bubble can seem. For three to four short months starting in November 1636, demand for tulip bulbs in Holland rocketed. For the rarer bulbs, price rises of up to 6,000 per cent were recorded. One bulb was particularly prized—the bulb from the exotic Semper Augustus tulip, exotically variegated, thanks to a virus, and beautiful. At the height of the mania, a Semper Augustus bulb could cost as much as a three-storey house in central Amsterdam. Bust followed boom, dramatically. By February 1637, most bulbs were impossible to sell, even at low prices, and many of the tulip speculators lost their fortunes. However, Tulipmania was not a one-off: there are many, many other examples of speculative bubbles throughout history—the South Sea Bubble of the 18th century, the rampant speculation in the US ending in the Great Crash of 1929, the dot.com bubble of the late 1990s, and the sub-prime crisis that precipitated the global financial crises in 2007/8 are just a few.

In explaining this sort of financial instability Keynes's ideas inspired a range of economists to develop richer models of financial markets, including Hyman Minsky as a notable example. Minsky developed a theory of credit cycles to capture some of the financial instability described earlier. Some of Hyman Minsky's work was particularly prescient in terms of predicting the 2007/8 financial crisis and its real impacts in terms of precipitating global recession. As with Keynes, emotional factors play an important role in Minsky's analysis of fragile financial systems and the implications of this financial fragility for the macroeconomy more widely. Minsky explained how business cycles are driven by cycles of fear and panic, with the fragility of the financial system playing a key role in driving extreme fluctuations. Minsky argued that the business cycle is driven, at first, by waves of speculative euphoria and entrepreneurs' over-optimism. Banks are lending too much. Businesses are borrowing too much. Eventually someone realizes that the boom has no stable foundation and interest rates start to rise, precipitating a bust phase as spectacular as the boom that preceded it.

Financial speculation leads to financial instability more generally, and these financial influences can have a detrimental impact on the macroeconomy. These messages have been popularized by Hollywood, most recently in the movie *The Big Short*. This tells the stories of financial traders who realized that enormous financial fragility was building up as complex new financial products were being developed, designed to make money by enabling people with poor credit ratings to take on multiple mortgages. This was the start of the *sub-prime mortgage crisis*. Even as they were making millions of dollars for themselves, the traders recognized that they were profiting on the backs of the many who would lose their homes and/or jobs because the financial instability would have such devastating impacts, not only on the US economy, but also on macroeconomic performance across the globe. As captured by Figure 6, the likely outcome was that, as people could no longer afford their mortgages, they would accumulate credit card debt and this would affect banks and other financial institutions, not only in the US but throughout the world.

Sub-prime mortgages mess

These ideas have been developed by a few economists. Robert Shiller has written much about 'irrational exuberance' (the term coined by Alan Greenspan, former chairman of the US Federal Reserve) in financial markets and its likely impact on employment, investment, output, and economic growth. Hersh Shefrin argues that irrational exuberance in bullish financial markets reflects interactions between fear, hope, and greed. A lot of what drives financial instability is about excessive risk-taking and emotions play their role in this—linking to George Loewenstein and others' insights about visceral factors, explored in Chapter 7. Loewenstein argues that the feeling of riskiness is linked to our emotional states, not to simple, stable preferences, as is usually assumed by economists.

6. Sub-prime mortgages mess.

Moods and the business cycle

Another perspective taken by behavioural macroeconomists is to
analyse the impact of confidence and social mood on macroeconomic
outcomes. Common factors may drive everyone's mood—for example,
most of us are in a more cheerful mood when the sun is shining.
Economists have used this insight to capture the connections
between moods and macroeconomic and financial fluctuations at
various stages of the business cycle.

Mark Kamstra and colleagues used data on seasonal depression to
test their hypothesis that financial markets move differently in
winter versus summer months. Seasonal depression can be

measured using the incidence of Seasonal Affective Disorder (SAD). People experiencing SAD are more likely to be cautious and risk-averse. If this translates through to financial market traders too, then they will be more risk-averse in the winter and also if they live in countries with fewer hours of sunlight. Kamstra and his team found that hours of darkness, cloud cover, and temperature all had a strong impact on stock market performance. They concluded that seasonal depression was increasing traders' risk-aversion. Kamstra's evidence was confirmed in a similar study conducted by David Hirshleifer and Tyler Shumway (2003). They also found that stock market performance correlates positively with hours of sunshine.

Some analysts believe that moods collectively experienced are the key macroeconomic driver, the ultimate explanatory variable. Robert Prechter and his team from the Socionomics Institute apply this insight to the analysis of financial market fluctuations. Prechter argues that *social mood* is the ultimate causal factor and the most powerful driver of macroeconomic trends. Resonating with Keynes and his analysis of the link between financial market fluctuations and real economic performance, Prechter asserts that the stock market captures our unconscious social mood. Prechter argues that this social mood drives buoyant phases of the macroeconomic cycle. When people are feeling more buoyant and optimistic, the positive social mood has a widespread impact—music is more 'pop-y', hemlines go up, and incumbent politicians do well. A buoyant stock market is also the best time for an incumbent president to go for re-election. But when the social mood is negative and pessimistic, financial markets are unstable, fashion is conservative, and music is depressive. The macroeconomy responds to social mood because social mood drives consumers' decisions and companies' business plans. Negative social mood also feeds into government policy-making: government is insular, favouring policies such as protectionism. All these different facets of a negative social mood then feed into a recessionary macroeconomy.

Happiness and well-being

Another theme in behavioural economics takes a different perspective entirely. Behavioural economists are also developing new ways of defining and measuring macroeconomic performance. Traditionally, statisticians in government departments collect information to measure macroeconomic performance overall, often using output/income measured in money terms (e.g. prices and average wages) as well as other objective measures of performance, including numbers of employed versus unemployed people.

Rather than focusing on fluctuations in monetary measures of macroeconomic performance in terms of the monetary value of output and production as measured by gross domestic product (GDP), behavioural economists also look at the psychological aspects of happiness and well-being.

One problem with measuring happiness and well-being is that our perceptions of our own happiness are dependent on context, and this links to the ideas of reference dependence explored in Chapters 4 and 5. Most measures of happiness and well-being are based on surveys—and self-reported levels of happiness can be like a snapshot taken at an unlikely moment. Questions asked before we decide how happy we are (or not) can be used as *priming* questions. For example, students' self-reported happiness can be manipulated by asking them to think about recent events. In one set of experiments students were asked priming questions such as 'Did you have a date last night?' 'Did it go well?'—these questions were designed to prime students to feel particular emotions, depending on how they had got on the previous night. The students' self-reported happiness changed according to the ordering of the questions. Students asked to state how happy they were *after* being asked questions about how things went last night reported different happiness levels. If they had had a miserable night before, then they recorded much lower levels of happiness. If they had had a good night, then they recorded relatively high levels of happiness. On the other hand, students' stated happiness levels were affected less by last night's events if they were asked about their happiness *before* they were asked questions about how they got on the previous night. Prompts to remember recent events were changing students' perceptions of their own happiness. So, whilst policy-makers should worry more about broader definitions of well-being, using happiness surveys is problematic because our self-reported happiness levels can be distorted by ephemeral factors.

Capturing this changing focus in macroeconomics towards broader measures of macroeconomic performance, the Legatum Institute, a London-based political/economic think-tank, released a report in 2014 setting out in detail the literature exploring how our well-being, happiness, and life satisfaction are driven by a wide range of socio-psychological, as well as economic and financial factors. This report also analyses new data sources to measure happiness and well-being, as well as providing some insight into how to analyse these data using robust econometric techniques.

Behavioural economists' interest in happiness and well-being has translated across into developing these new sources of macroeconomic data around the world. Public health data can also be a useful indicator of collective mood—for example, data on suicide rates, mental illness, and stress-related illness. A wide range of national and international statistical agencies are now collecting data on happiness, well-being, and life satisfaction—for example, via household surveys including questions about subjective well-being alongside the standard labour force survey questions about employment and unemployment.

The Office of National Statistics in the UK is now including responses to questions about life satisfaction in its household surveys. Other countries from China to France are collecting similar data, and the OECD is collating international data sets. Potentially these new data can be fed into macroeconomic analyses capturing a more nuanced and wide-ranging picture of macroeconomic performance. Perhaps most influentially, the World Bank is now releasing an annual *World Happiness Report*, which should give behavioural macroeconomists some useful data to capture how macroeconomic trends in happiness shift across space and over time, as well as opportunities to connect these new happiness and well-being measures with more conventional measures of macroeconomic performance.

Technological innovations are also helpful in collecting better behavioural macroeconomic data. Behavioural researchers can now implement wide-scale online surveys and they can use text messaging and social media to collect data too (e.g. from Google searches, Twitter feeds, and Facebook 'likes'). With the growth of these types of 'Big Data', some of the gaps in the behavioural macroeconomists' data sets can potentially be filled.

Using subjective data is problematic, but with the cooperation of economists, statisticians, and government this area is increasingly gaining credibility. Capturing well-being data is also problematic, and much more research is needed to assess the pros and cons of these new statistics, as well as to explore some of the other ways in which behavioural macroeconomists can better understand and measure happiness and well-being.

Chapter 9
Economic behaviour and public policy

At its best, economics can help policy-makers to design policies to resolve a wide range of economic and financial problems, both for individual people and for economies as a whole too. Conventional economic policies focus on resolving market failures: if markets are not working well and prices are not effectively signalling information about relative supply and demand, then government policy instruments can help to resolve the problems that emerge as a consequence. In this chapter we will explore some key insights and evidence from behavioural public policy, focusing on microeconomic policy. Developing a set of coherent behavioural macroeconomic policy tools is a much more complicated challenge, which, so far at least, has not yet been properly attempted.

Microeconomic policy

Traditionally, taxes and subsidies have been the main policy instruments used by governments and policy-makers to help markets work better. A well-trodden example is smoking. If smoking imposes costs on the tax-payer in terms of strains on the public health system, then taxing cigarettes helps—not only to reduce the incentive to smoke, but also in providing governments with revenue to pay for their health systems. On the other hand, if, for example, a particular region of a country is suffering from industrial decline then subsidies can be used to encourage economic activity in that area.

Taxes and subsidies suffer from a range of practical, technical, and logistical limitations and so modern economic policy covers a wider range of economic instruments too, including instruments inspired by Nobel laureate Ronald Coase's analyses of market transactions. Coase's insights underlie the design of artificial trading systems, which can be created to address problems emerging when prices provide imperfect signals of supply and demand. These artificial markets replace 'missing markets'—markets that are missing because market prices exclude them. Pollution is a simple example. When a business pollutes the air or water, if nothing is done about that then the business is polluting for free—they do not have to compensate anyone for the negative consequences of their pollution. As such, the market for pollution is missing.

A solution based on Coase's insights is to develop an artificial market—in the last case, this could take the form of emissions trading schemes. People and businesses can buy and sell rights to pollute (or to be polluted). Creating these artificial markets is not straightforward, but overall, like taxes and subsidies, they are about resolving market and institutional failures rather than individuals' behaviours.

What is behavioural public policy? Nudging for behaviour change

Behavioural public policy looks at these problems from a different perspective. Instead of focusing on market failures, it focuses on *behaviour change*—that is, changing the way that people make their everyday decisions and choices by nudging them towards more efficient and productive decision-making.

The seminal book in the area is Thaler and Sunstein's book *Nudge*—and UK policy-makers often cite *Mindspace*, the essential nsights of which are similar to those in *Nudge*. Thaler and Sunstein draw on the large literature from behavioural economics and psychology more generally, especially the ideas about choice overload, information load, heuristics, and behavioural biases, which are covered here in Chapters 4 and 5. They argue that, in designing effective policy instruments, policy-makers need to understand the heuristics and biases driving people's decisions. Then the structure of people's decision-making can be redesigned. This insight forms the foundation of what Thaler and Sunstein call our *choice architecture*. How are our choices structured? How do we process information before deciding what we want to do and buy? Can our decision-making processes be redesigned?

Thaler and Sunstein argue that if policy-makers can better understand people's choice architecture then they can design policies to help people decide more effectively. Giving people simple choices, designing prompts and nudges to lead people's decisions in more constructive and positive directions, giving frequent feedback so that 'good' decisions are reinforced and 'bad' decisions are discouraged—all these strategies form part of behavioural public policy-makers' tool-kits.

Thaler and Sunstein argue that, politically and morally, using nudges is a form of *libertarian paternalism*. People retain power over their own choices so it is libertarian, but it also incorporates *nudges* from government, and in this sense it is paternalistic. In other words, it is libertarian in the sense that people still have a choice; it is paternalistic in the sense that it is a government intervention. Thaler and Sunstein suggest that nudging combines the best of both worlds (though their critics would argue that it combines the worst of both worlds). Taxes and subsidies impose costs and benefits on different groups of people. Generally, an ordinary person cannot choose whether or not to pay taxes (though people and businesses able to pay for expensive accountants may have more control over this). We cannot easily choose whether or not we receive a subsidy, but Thaler and

Sunstein argue that nudges can be designed to allow people some choice, for example via clever design of default options.

Nudging in practice: default options

What do nudges involve in practice? Many nudges are based around the manipulation of *default options*. These are used to leverage a particular type of behavioural bias—the status quo bias—explored in Chapters 4 and 5. If a policy-maker (or business) sets up the default option (the option a person ends up with if they do nothing at all) then a surprisingly large proportion of people will stick with this default option. There is a range of reasons for this. People tend to favour the status quo. They are not always quick to move away from it because changing choices can be risky and/or involve effort. People may interpret the default option as a type of signal about what is the best choice for them. If a default option is set to match the most constructive decision, then more people are likely, albeit passively, to take that decision.

To illustrate with an example, how to encourage people to donate their organs represents a big problem in most countries. The demand for organs is much, much greater than the supply. There are policy dilemmas in this area too—for example, around the ethics of paying people to donate organs—but here we will concentrate on how a behavioural public policy-maker might respond. The policy-maker could set up the default option so that the default is to donate organs. If a person does not want to do this then they would have the option to opt out. In this way, the individual retains her freedom to choose.

Default options can also be used to help us save more for our pensions. In Chapter 4, we covered Benartzi and Thaler's 'Save More for Tomorrow' pension scheme, which also exploits default options. In order to encourage employees to save more for their retirement, the default option in this scheme is that a fixed proportion of all salary goes into an employee's pension pot, with the amount increasing alongside any salary rises. But employees are not forced to do this—they have a choice. They can opt-out. The default option is the policy-maker's tool—this is the paternalistic part of the nudge. The opt-out is the decision-maker's choice—this is the libertarian part of the nudge.

One problem with these types of nudges is that they are often exploited by commercial businesses too, to our detriment. A marketing business wanting to make some extra money from harvesting and selling our contact details to other businesses can set up their contact detail forms so that we do not notice we have given them permission to circulate our contact details. They understand our choice architecture too well.

Switching

Related to default options is the problem of infrequent switching, as also mentioned in Chapter 4. We stick with an energy supplier, a mobile phone company, or a bank for many years, even when the deal they give us is very poor value. We are slow to switch supplier. For energy switching in the UK, in 2016 Ofgem (Great Britain's energy market regulator) reported that over 60 per cent of consumers do not recall switching energy suppliers even though by doing so they could have saved £200 on their annual energy bills. The problem with our low levels of switching is that it lessens the competitive pressure on businesses: if they do not lose customers when they offer a bad value deal, what is their incentive to offer a better deal? Low levels of switching also reflect a status quo bias and, increasingly, government policy-makers are working on encouraging us to switch more frequently if we are not getting a good deal from a supplier. The tools they are designing to encourage more switching are also focused on a better understanding of choice architecture—for example, by making it easier for us to switch or by reducing the problems of choice overload and/or information load that make switching supplier a cognitive challenge. This increased emphasis by policy-makers on encouraging us to switch has had some success in the UK. There is some evidence that these policies are working with switching rates increasing. Ofgem reported that 2015 energy supplier switching rates by households were 15 per cent higher than in 2014.

Social nudges

Another powerful nudge devised by policy-makers harnesses our susceptibility to social influence, building on the ideas outlined in Chapter 3. In the energy sector, some important findings relate to household energy consumption, based on findings from a relatively large body of academic studies. For example, Wesley Schultz and colleagues analysed households in California. The householders were given two types of information. The first set of information related to the energy consumption of other households in a given neighbourhood. This gave householders a social reference point against which they could compare their own energy consumption. Harnessing Thaler and Sunstein's ideas about designing a choice architecture in which choices are simplified, social approval/disapproval for a household's consumption relative to the neighbourhood average was conveyed via a smiley face, if consumption was below the local social average—or a frowny face, if it was above the local social average. The second set of information was a set of instructions about how to reduce energy consumption.

What impact do these different types of information have? To test the differential effectiveness of the various types of information, one group of experimental participants (a control group) were only given energy saving tips. Another group (a treatment group) were given information about social averages too. The researchers found that the social nudges were powerful—the householders in the treatment group, with the social information, were more likely to adjust their energy towards the average than the householders in the control group, adjusting their consumption downwards

...en told that their consumption was above average for their neighbourhood. Researchers inferred that this was because householders were adjusting their choices towards a social norm or reference point. A wide range of similar studies has captured similar findings, and these insights have been incorporated into new designs for energy bills—for example the OPower bills illustrated in Figure 7.

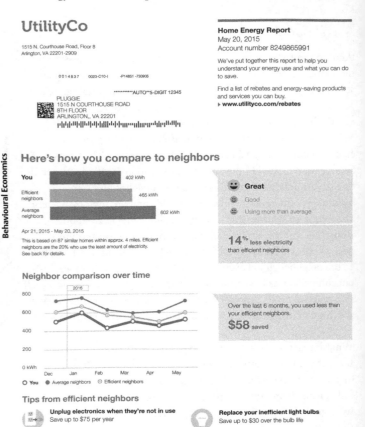

7. Social nudges for saving energy.

A key lesson for policy-makers, however, is to beware the unintended consequences. Researchers identified *boomerang effects*: householders whose energy consumption was below the neighbourhood average tended to be encouraged by social information about neighbours' higher consumption to consume *more* not less. If the distribution of energy consumption across households is symmetric, then perhaps as many people will be adjusting their energy consumption upwards towards the social average as are adjusting their energy consumption downwards. If this is the case, then the average consumption will not change and the policy will have been pointless.

Other policy initiatives

More and more often, behavioural public policy principles are extending to other areas of public policy. For example, the findings about social nudges in the energy sector have spread to taxation. In Chapter 3, we noted how social influences can be harnessed by tax officials and, in the UK, Her Majesty's Revenue and Customs (HMRC) has trialled sending letters to people who are late paying their tax bills, informing them that some proportion of other people have paid their bills on time. The idea here is to use social pressure as a persuasive instrument. This type of social nudge has reportedly been successful in the UK, and in other countries too. Other policy-makers are using default options and other insights to supplement more conventional policies in areas such as competition policy and financial services too.

It is important however, that policy-makers do not lose sight of conventional economic policies—and some of the most effective policy initiatives combine standard economic policy tools with behavioural embellishments. Other policies combine behavioural insights with classic approaches to designing effective incentives. One example is the policy of charging for plastic bags—a policy implemented in Ireland many years ago, to

8. **Plastic bag littering.**

overcome the problem of plastic bag littering—as illustrated in Figure 8.

Plastic bag littering is a significant environmental problem and has devastating effects for wildlife, the environment, and human health. There is some evidence that our water supplies are becoming contaminated with tiny remnants of all the plastic bags which we carelessly throw away. Manufacturing plastic bags also involves negative impacts from pollution and the excessive use of scarce non-renewable resources. When the UK government introduced a 5 pence (p) plastic bag charge in 2015, stories started circulating that, in some homes, the bags were worth more than people's houses—because people had accumulated so many bags that were now worth 5p each.

More seriously, the 5p charge is an illustration of how insights from behavioural economics can inform the design of conventional economic policies while also promoting behaviour change. The 5p charge is a tax, but one designed to correct a behavioural bias not a market failure (assuming that it is not particularly rational to hoard large numbers of actually almost valueless plastic bags). Perhaps hoarding of plastic bags is a demonstration of the endowment effect—we over-value things we already own. Whatever the underlying psychological reasons may be for plastic bag hoarding, a conventional tax can be used to nudge us away from either accumulating a load of plastic bags that are useless to us or using too many and then throwing them away. But, again, there were unintended consequences and there is some evidence that the overall usage of plastic bags did not decrease. Many people were no longer re-using ordinary plastic supermarket bags as bin bags. Instead they were increasing their purchases of other, bigger plastic bags, including 'bags for life' and heavy-duty bin bags, thus negating some (possibly all) of the positive environmental impacts expected from the 5p bag charge.

The future of policy

The future for behavioural public policy is promising. Spinouts from government policy units have done well, perhaps most famously the Behavioural Insights team originally part of former UK prime minister David Cameron's Cabinet office, nicknamed the 'Nudge Unit'. The Nudge Unit is doing extremely well commercially, and is the focus of a lot of public attention, positive and negative, and on a national and international scale.

There are dangers, however. Behavioural public policy has become very fashionable but, as with all fashions, it does generate excessive hype and is vulnerable to a backlash. Also, a lot of excitement has been generated around behavioural insights and policies based around nudging. More evidence is needed about how effective and how 'sticky' these policy interventions really are. Can we establish using robust statistical analyses that these nudges are really effective, and at a large scale? Can the positive impacts identified so far be replicated across a wider range of studies? Are nudge policies just gimmicky policies with short-run impacts that quickly disappear? For those on whom nudges have been tried, do they eventually return to their old habits and choices? Or do behavioural policy nudges have stronger, more long-lasting impacts?

In ensuring that the most profound behavioural policy lessons endure, it will be important to build a robust and scientifically rigorous body of evidence that demonstrates not only when and where the policies are working, but also when and where they *do not* work. The problem for much academic research is that negative results are not easy to publish. A finding that a policy intervention has not worked is not nearly so exciting and interesting to read about as a finding that a policy intervention has had an amazingly positive benefit. Behavioural economics tells us that we tend to over-weight the information that is most memorable, and the same is true of behavioural public policy evidence.

Another pitfall for policy-makers will emerge if they are distracted away from the conventional economic policies that have been shown to work well in resolving market and institutional failures. Nudging is fashionable in policy circles, but has it led to a neglect of the traditional policy instruments that can effectively address failures in markets and other institutions? Nudges address people's biases and mistakes, but helping people to decide more effectively will not remove market and institutional failures. In the future, policy-makers need to look carefully at how policies based around behavioural insights can be used to complement rather than replace conventional economic policy instruments. In this scenario, a key policy question will be how to coordinate conventional and behavioural policies more effectively, without disproportionately favouring one over the other. If we can get this policy balance right, then behavioural economics will give us some powerful tools to resolve a much wider range of market failures and behavioural biases, with positive benefits for individuals, economies, and society.

References and further reading

Chapter 1: Economics and behaviour

There are many introductions to behavioural economics, including:

Ariely, D. (2008) *Predictably Irrational—The Hidden Forces that Shape Our Decisions*, New York: Harper Collins.

Gigerenzer, G. (2014) *Risk Savvy: How to Make Good Decisions*, London: Penguin Books.

Kahneman, D. (2011) *Thinking, Fast and Slow*, London: Allen Lane.

Thaler, R. H. (2015) *Misbehaving: The Making of Behavioural Economics*, London: Allen Lane.

For more academic introductions, which assume a background knowledge of economics, see:

Baddeley, M. (2013) *Behavioural Economics and Finance*, Routledge: Abingdon.

Earl, P. E. and Kemp, S. (1999) *The Elgar Companion to Consumer Research and Economic Psychology*, Cheltenham: Edward Elgar.

Laibson, D. and List, J. E. (2015) Principles of (behavioral) economics, *American Economic Review* 105(5): 385–90.

There is a large literature on rationality in economics, for example, see:

Simon, H. A. (1955) A behavioural model of rational choice, *Quarterly Journal of Economics* 69: 99–118.

Leibenstein, H. (1976) *Beyond Economic Man*, Cambridge, MA: Harvard University Press.

th, V. L. (2003) Constructivist and ecological rationality in economics, *American Economic Review* 93(3): 465–508.

apter 2: Motivation and incentives

behavioural economists' analyses of incentives and tivation, see:

Ariely, D. A., Bracha, A., and Meier, S. (2009) Doing good or doing well? Image motivation and monetary incentives in behaving prosocially, *American Economic Review* 99(1): 544–55.

Bénabou, R. and Tirole, J. (2006) Incentives and prosocial behavior, *American Economic Review* 96(5): 1652–78.

Frey, B. S. and Jegen, R. (2001) How intrinsic motivation is crowded out and in, *Journal of Economic Surveys* 15(5): 589–611.

For analyses of social incentives and gift exchange in labour markets, see:

Akerlof, G. A. (1982) Labor contracts as partial gift exchange, *Quarterly Journal of Economics* 97(4): 543–69.

The nursery school study described in this chapter is explained in detail in:

Gneezy, U. and Rustichini, A. (2000) A fine is a price, *Journal of Legal Studies* 29(1): 1–17.

Chapter 3: Social lives

Some seminal papers on social preferences and related experimental studies include:

Berg, J. E., Dikhaut, J., and McCabe, K. (1995) Trust, reciprocity and social history, *Games and Economic Behavior* 10(1): 122–42.

Fehr, E. and Gächter, S. (2000) Cooperation and punishment in public goods experiments, *American Economic Review* 90(4): 980–94.

Fehr, E. and Schmidt, K. M. (1999) Theory of fairness, competition and cooperation, *Quarterly Journal of Economics* 114(3): 817–68.

Güth, W., Schmittberger, R., and Schwarze, B. (1982) An experimental analysis of ultimatum bargaining, *Journal of Economic Behavior and Organisation* 3: 367–88.

Henrich, J., Boyd, R., Bowles, S., Camerer, C., Fehr, E., Gintis, H., and McElreath, R. (2001) In search of *homo economicus*: behavioral experiments in 15 small-scale societies, *American Economic Review* 91(2): 73–8.

For more detail on neuroeconomic studies of herding, see:

Baddeley, M. (2010) Herding, social influence and economic decision-making: socio-psychological and neuroscientific analyses, *Philosophical Transactions of the Royal Society B* 365(1538): 281–90.

Singer, T. and Fehr, E. (2005) The neuroeconomics of mind reading and empathy, *American Economic Review* 95(2): 340–5.

From economics, the seminal papers on herding and social learning include:

Anderson, L. and Holt, C. (1996) Classroom games: information cascades, *Journal of Economic Perspectives* 10(4): 187–93.

Banerjee, A. (1992) A simple model of herd behavior, *Quarterly Journal of Economics* 107(3): 797–817.

Bikhchandani, S., Hirshleifer, D., and Welch, I. (1998) Learning from the behavior of others: conformity, fads, and informational cascades, *Journal of Economic Perspectives* 12(3): 151–70.

Jan Surowiecki has written an excellent lay-person's introduction:

Surowiecki, J. (2004) *The Wisdom of Crowds: Why the Many Are Smarter than the Few*, London: Abacus.

For an analysis of herding in scientific research and expert opinion, see:

Baddeley, M. (2015) Herding, social influences and behavioural bias in scientific research, *European Molecular Biology Organisation Reports* 16(8): 902–5.

Baddeley, M. (2013) Herding, social influence and expert opinion, *Journal of Economic Methodology* 20(1): 37–45.

For an early analysis of mirror neurons and imitation, see:

Rizzolati, G. and Craighero, L. (2004) The mirror neuron system, *Annual Reviews of Neuroscience* 27:169–92.

For more on identity in behavioural economics, see:

Akerlof, G. A. and Kranton, R. E. (2011) *Identity Economics—How our Identities Shape Our Work, Wages and Wellbeing*, Princeton: Princeton University Press.

Solomon Asch's original line experiments to capture group influence are described in:

Asch, S. E. (1955) Opinions and social pressure, *Scientific American* 193(5): 31–5.

Chapter 4: Quick thinking

The choice experiments from this chapter are described in:

Iyengar, S. and Lepper, M. (2000) When choice is demotivating, *Journal of Personality and Social Psychology* 79(6): 995–1006.

The evidence about choice overload is mixed, and for some meta-analyses of the evidence, see:

Chernev, A., Böckenholt, U., and Goodman, J. (2015) Choice overload: A conceptual review and meta-analysis, *Journal of Consumer Psychology* 25(2): 333–58.
Scheibehenne, B., Greifeneder, R., and Todd, P. M. (2010) Can there ever be too many options? A meta-analytic review of choice overload, *Journal of Consumer Research* 37(3): 409–25.

For Kahneman and Tversky's seminal paper on heuristics and bias, see:

Tversky, A. and Kahneman, D. (1974) Judgement under uncertainty: Heuristics and biases, *Science* 185: 1124–31.

On cognitive dissonance, see:

Akerlof, G. A. and Dickens, W. T. (1982) The economic consequences of cognitive dissonance, *American Economic Review* 72(3): 307–19.

For Thaler and Benartzi's application of default options, see:

Thaler, R. H. and Benartzi, S. (2004) Save More Tomorrow™: using behavioral economics to increase employee saving, *Journal of Political Economy* 112(1): S164–S187.

Chapter 5: Risky choices

The seminal paper on prospect theory is:

Kahneman, D. and Tversky, A. (1979) Prospect theory—an analysis of decision under risk, *Econometrica* 47(2): 263–92.

Regret theory is introduced in:

Loomes, G. and Sugden, R. (1982) Regret theory: an alternative theory of choice under uncertainty, *Economic Journal* 92(368): 805–24.

The other research on loss aversion, endowment effects, and status quo bias referred to in this chapter includes:

Kahneman, D., Knetsch, J., and Thaler, R. (1991) Anomalies: The endowment effect, loss aversion and status quo bias, *Journal of Economic Perspectives* 5(1): 193–206.

Viscusi, W. Kip, Magat, W. A., and Huber, J. (1987) An investigation of the rationality of consumer valuations of multiple health risks, *Rand Journal of Economics* 18(4): 465–79.

Chapter 6: Taking time

The seminal papers on time discounting cited in this chapter include research from neuroscience and behavioural ecology, as well as behavioural economics and economic psychology. The studies and analyses cited include:

Ainslie, G. (1974) Impulse control in pigeons, *Journal of the Experimental Analysis of Behavior* 21(3): 485–9.

Angeletos, G.-M., Laibson, D., Repetto, A., Tobacman, J., and Weinberg, S. (2001) The hyperbolic consumption model: Calibration, simulation, and empirical evaluation, *Journal of Economic Perspectives* 15(3): 47–68.

Camerer, C. F., Babcock, L., Loewenstein, G., and Thaler, R. H. (1997) Labour supply of New York City cab drivers: One day at a time, *Quarterly Journal of Economics* 112(2): 407–41.

DellaVigna, S. and Malmendier, U. (2006) Paying not to go to the gym, *American Economic Review* 96(3): 694–719.

Duflo, E., Kremer, M., and Robinson, J. (2011) Nudging farmers to use fertilizer: Theory and experimental evidence from Kenya, *American Economic Review* 101(6): 2350–90.

Glimcher, P. W., Kable, J., and Louie, K. (2007) Neuroeconomic studies of impulsivity: No or just as soon as possible, *American Economic Review* 97(2): 142–7.

Laibson, D. (1997) Golden eggs and hyperbolic discounting, *Quarterly Journal of Economics* 112: 443–78.

McClure, S. M., Laibson, D. I., Loewenstein, G., and Cohen, J. D. (2004) Separate neural systems value immediate and delayed rewards, *Science* 306: 503–7.

Mischel, W., Shoda, Y., and Rodriguez, M. L. (1989) Delay of gratification in children, *Science* 244(4907): 933–8.

Mulcahy, N. J. and Call, J. (2006) Apes save tools for future use, *Science* 312: 1038–40.

O'Donoghue, T. and Rabin, M. (2001) Choice and procrastination, *Quarterly Journal of Economics* 116(1): 121–60.

Read, D., Loewenstein, G., and Montague, M. (1999) Choice bracketing, *Journal of Risk and Uncertainty* 19(1–3): 171–97.

Rick, S. and Loewenstein, G. (2008) Intangibility in in temporal choice, *Philosophical Transactions of the Royal Society B*, 363(1511): 3813–24.

Strotz, R. H. (1955) Myopia and inconsistency in dynamic utility maximization, *Review of Economic Studies* 23: 165–80.

Thaler, R. H. (1999) Mental accounting matters, *Journal of Behavioral Decision Making* 12: 183–206.

Warner, J. T. and Pleeter, S. (2001) The personal discount rate: Evidence from military downsizing programs, *American Economic Review* 91(1): 33–53.

Chapter 7: Personalities, moods, and emotions

For an account of the Big Five personality tests and the cognitive reflexivity test (CRT), see:

Frederick, S. (2005) Cognitive reflection and decision-making, *Journal of Economic Perspectives* 19(4): 25–42.

McCrae, R. R. and Costa, P. T. (1987) Validation of the five-factor model of personality across instruments and observers, *Journal of Personality and Social Psychology* 52: 81–90.

The answer to the 'bats and balls' CRT question is that the ball costs 5 cents.

On impacts of incentives on experimental participants' responses, see:

Gneezy, U. and Rustichini, A. (2000) Pay enough or don't pay at all, *Quarterly Journal of Economics* 115(3): 791–810.

For some of David Cesarini and colleagues' research into genetics and personality, see:

Cesarini, D., Dawes, C. T., Johannesson, M., Lichtenstein, P., and Wallace, B. (2009) Genetic variation in preferences for giving and risk taking, *Quarterly Journal of Economics* 124(2): 809–42.

For other references to research on personality and economic life chances, see:

Borghans, L., Duckworth, A. L., Heckman, J. J., and Ter Weel, B. (2008) The economics and psychology of personality traits, *Journal of Human Resources* 43(4): 972–1059.

Heckman, J., Moon, S. H., Pinto, R., Savelyev, P., and Yavitz, A. (2010) The rate of return to the HighScope Perry Preschool Program, *Journal of Public Economics* 94(1–2): 114–28.

Mischel, W., Shoda, Y., and Rodriguez, M. L. (1989) Delay of gratification in children, *Science* 244(4907): 933–1038.

For the references cited relating to emotions, see:

Elster, J. (1998) Emotions and economic theory, *Journal of Economic Literature* 36(1): 47–74.

le Doux, J. E. (1996) *The Emotional Brain*, New York: Simon & Schuster.

For Dan Ariely's work with colleagues on emotions and preferences, see:

Lee, L., Amir, O., and Ariely, D. (2009) In search of homo economicus: Cognitive noise and the role of emotion in preference consistency, *Journal of Consumer Research* 36(2): 173–87.

The literature on addiction is a response to Gary Becker's rational addiction model:

Becker, G. S. and Murphy, K. M. (1988) A theory of rational addiction, *Journal of Political Economy* 96(4): 675–700.

Behavioural economists' alternative analyses of addiction include:

Baddeley, M. (2013) Bad habits, *Behavioural Economics and Finance*, Routledge: Abingdon, chapter 10.

Bernheim, B. D. and Rangel, A. (2004) Addiction and cue-triggered decision processes, *American Economic Review* 94(5): 1558–90.

Laibson, D. I. (2001) A cue-theory of consumption, *Quarterly Journal of Economics* 116(1): 81–119.

Loewenstein, G. (1996) Out of control: Visceral influences on decision making, *Organizational Behavior and Human Decision Processes* 65(3): 272–92.

Camerer et al.'s survey papers are good introductions to neuroeconomics, for example, see:

Camerer, C. F., Loewenstein, G., and Prelec, D. (2005)
     Neuroeconomics: How neuroscience can inform economics,
     Journal of Economic Literature 43(1): 9–64.

For introductions to dual systems models and the somatic marker
hypothesis, see:

Damasio, A. R. (1994) *Descartes' Error: Emotion, Reason, and the
     Human Brain*, London: Vintage.
Kahneman, D. (2003) Maps of bounded rationality: Psychology for
     behavioral economics, *American Economic Review* 93(5):
     1449–75.
Kahneman, D. (2011) *Thinking, Fast and Slow*, London: Allen Lane.

For the neuroeconomic analyses of emotions in economics and finance
cited in this chapter, see:

Coates, J. M. and Herbert, J. (2008) Endogenous steroids and
     financial risk taking on a London trading floor, *Proceedings of the
     National Academy of Sciences* 105(16): 6167–72.
Cohen, J. D. (2005) The vulcanization of the human brain: A neural
     perspective on interactions between cognition and emotion,
     Journal of Economic Perspectives 19(4): 3–24.
Knutson, B. and Bossaerts, P. (2007) Neural antecedents of financial
     decisions, *Journal of Neuroscience* 27(31): 8174–7.
Kuhnen, C. and Knutson, B. (2005) The neural basis of financial risk
     taking, *Neuron* 47(5): 763–70.
Lo, A. W. and Repin, D. V. (2002) The psychophysiology of real-time
     financial risk processing, *Journal of Cognitive Neuroscience* 14(3):
     323–39.
Sanfey, A. G., Rilling, J. K., Aronson, J. A., Nystrom, L. E., and Cohen,
     J. D. (2003) The neural basis of economic decision-making in the
     Ultimatum Game, *Science* 300: 1755–8.
Shiv, B., Loewenstein, G., Bechara, A., Damasio, H., and Damasio, A.
     R. (2005) Investment behaviour and the negative side of emotion,
     Psychological Science 16(6): 435–9.
Smith, K. and Dickhaut, J. (2005) Economics and emotions:
     Institutions matter, *Games and Economic Behavior* 52: 316–35.
Tuckett, D. (2011) *Minding the Markets: An Emotional Finance View
     of Financial Instability*, Basingstoke: Palgrave Macmillan.

Chapter 8: Behaviour in the macroeconomy

Important early writings in behavioural macroeconomics include:

Katona, G. (1975) *Psychological Economics*, New York: Elsevier.

Keynes, J. M. (1936) *The General Theory of Employment, Interest and Money*, London: Macmillan, especially chapter 12.

Minsky, H. (1986) *Stabilizing an Unstable Economy*, New Haven, CT: Yale University Press.

George Akerlof covered many of the key themes in his Nobel Prize lecture:

Akerlof, G. (2002) Behavioral macroeconomics and macroeconomic behavior, *American Economic Review* 92(3): 411–33.

Tali Sharot has done some interesting research on optimism bias, introduced in:

Sharot, T. (2011) *The Optimism Bias: Why We're Wired to Look on the Bright Side*, New York: Pantheon Books.

Other studies on optimism bias cited here include:

Ifcher, J. and Zarghamee, H. (2011) Happiness and time preference: The effect of positive affect in a random-assignment experiment, *American Economic Review* 101(7): 3109–29.

National Audit Office (2013) Over-optimism in government projects. Report by the UK's National Audit Office.

Some modern behavioural macroeconomic analyses and models include:

Akerlof, G. and Shiller, R. (2009) *Animal Spirits: How Human Psychology Drives the Economy and Why it Matters for Global Capitalism*, Princeton: Princeton University Press.

Baddeley, M. (2016) Behavioural macroeconomics: Time, optimism and animal spirits, in R. Frantz, S.-H. Chen, K. Dopfer, F. Heukelom, and S. Mousavi (eds), *Routledge Handbook of Behavioural Economics*, New York: Routledge, pp. 266–79.

de Grauwe, P. (2012) Booms and busts in economic activity: A behavioural explanation, *Journal of Economic Behavior and Organisation* 83(3): 484–501.

Farmer, R. E. A. (2012) Confidence, crashes and animal spirits, *Economic Journal* 122(559): 155–72.

Howitt, P. and McAfee, R. P. (1992) Animal spirits, *American Economic Review* 82(3): 493–507.

Woodford, M. (1990) Learning to believe in sunspots, *Econometrica* 58: 277–307.

For the analyses of financial market bubbles and instability, including the references mentioned in this chapter exploring how mood and weather might affect financial markets, see:

Hirshleifer, D. and Shumway, T. (2003) Good day sunshine: Stock returns and the weather, *Journal of Finance* 58(3): 1009–32.

Kamstra, M. J., Kramer, L. A., and Levi, M. D. (2003) Winter blues: A SAD stock market cycle, *American Economic Review* 93(1): 324–43.

Kindleberger, C. P. (2001) *Manias, Panics and Crashes: A History of Financial Crises* (4th edition), Hoboken, NJ: John Wiley.

For an introduction to Robert Prechter and others on social mood, see:

Casti, J. L. (2010) *Mood Matters: From Rising Skirt Lengths to the Collapse of World Powers*, Berlin: Springer-Verlag.

Some introductions to happiness and well-being include:

Haybron, D. M. (2013) *Happiness: A Very Short Introduction*, Oxford: Oxford University Press.

Layard, R. L. (2005) *Happiness: Lessons from a New Science*, London: Penguin.

O'Donnell, G., Deaton, A., Durand, M., Halpern, D., and Layard, R. (2014) *Wellbeing and Policy*, London: Legatum Institute.

Oswald, A. J., and Wu, S. (2010) Objective confirmation of subjective measures of human well-being: Evidence from the U.S.A., *Science* 327(5965): 576–79.

The World Bank, Happiness Report, various years, Washington, DC: World Bank. <http://worldhappiness.report>.

Chapter 9: Economic behaviour and public policy

Influential introductions to behavioural economics for policy-makers include:

Dolan, P., Hallsworth, M., Halpern, D., King, D., and Vlaev, I. (2010) *Mindspace—Influencing Behaviour Through Public Policy*, London: Cabinet Office/Institute for Government.

Schultz, P. W., Nolan, J. M., Cialdini, R. B., Goldstein, N. J., and Griskevicius, V. (2007) The constructive, destructive, and reconstructive power of social norms, *Psychological Science* 18(5): 429–34.

Thaler, R. and Sunstein, C. (2008) *Nudge—Improving Decisions about Health, Wealth and Happiness*, New Haven, CT: Yale University Press.

For a survey of behavioural economic insights around energy:

Baddeley, M. (2015) Behavioural approaches to managing household energy consumption, in F. Beckenbach and W. Kahlenborn (eds), *New Perspectives for Environmental Policies through Behavioural Economics*, Berlin: Springer, pp. 2013–235.

Also, Cass Sunstein has written deeply and thoughtfully about policy nudges built around default options:

Sunstein, C. (2015) *Choosing Not to Choose: Understanding the Value of Choice*, Oxford: Oxford University Press.

Index

Index